MODERN HUMANITIES RESEARCH ASSOCIATION
EUROPEAN TRANSLATIONS
VOLUME 2

GERMANIC EDITOR
RITCHIE ROBERTSON

LUISE GOTTSCHED
DER LOCKENRAUB

ALEXANDER POPE
THE RAPE OF THE LOCK

EDITED BY
HILARY BROWN

Luise Gottsched

Der Lockenraub

Alexander Pope

The Rape of the Lock

Edited by
Hilary Brown

Modern Humanities Research Association
2014

Published by

The Modern Humanities Research Association,
1 Carlton House Terrace
London SW1Y 5AF

First published 2014

ISBN 978-0-947623-84-5

Copies may be ordered from www.translations.mhra.org.uk

CONTENTS

INTRODUCTION

Luise Gottsched née Kulmus (1713–1762) is recognized as one of Germany's most significant early women of letters. She is best known for her work in the field of drama: she published four comedies, which are considered important for the development of the genre in Germany, and one tragedy, thought to be the first ever written by a German woman. Her play *Die Pietisterey im Fischbein-Rocke* (1736) is a minor classic. Gottsched is also becoming known as a translator, and in fact she dedicated most of her life to translation. *Die Pietisterey im Fischbein-Rocke*, often treated as an 'original' work, is actually an adaptation of a French play called *La Femme docteur ou la théologie tombée en quenouille* by one Guillaume-Hyacinthe Bougeant. Over the course of her career Gottsched produced or contributed to more than fifty volumes of translations, covering a range of genres and disciplines, from drama and poetry to philosophy, history, archaeology and even theoretical physics. She translated works by many key figures of the European Enlightenment, among them Molière, Voltaire, Emilie du Châtelet, François Fénelon and Bernhard le Bovier de Fontenelle. Her translations can be viewed as part of an ambitious, progressive programme undertaken with her husband, the Leipzig professor Johann Christoph Gottsched: it appears that she wanted to introduce her compatriots to new forms and ideas emanating from the republic of letters and to inspire the further development of German literature and culture.[1]

Der Lockenraub, Gottsched's translation of Alexander Pope's mock-heroic poem *The Rape of the Lock*, appeared in 1744 at a time when English literature was still relatively unfamiliar to readers in Germany. The educated classes had been in thrall to France and French culture for the last hundred years, awed by the power and prestige of the Bourbon monarchs and French culture of the golden age: they tended to speak and write in French, read French literature and watch French plays. Britain, in contrast, was still largely a *terra incognita*. In the first half of the eighteenth century, opportunities to learn English were few and far between; it was difficult to get hold of English-language books; and only a 'trickle' of English books found their way into Germany in translation — often

1. Some sections of this Introduction draw on material originally published in Hilary Brown, *Luise Gottsched the Translator* (Rochester, NY: Camden House, 2012), particularly pp. 143–52.

fewer than ten titles per year — with many being made from French translations rather than the English source texts.[2]

We might initially be surprised to find that it was Luise Gottsched whose name appears on the cover of *Der Lockenraub*. For the Gottscheds are probably thought of primarily as Francophiles. In their efforts to reform German culture in the early eighteenth century, it is well known that they frequently turned to the more established culture of their western neighbours for inspiration. In the field of drama, for instance, it is French classical and neo-classical playwrights such as Pierre Corneille and Philippe Néricault Destouches who provide texts and models for *Die deutsche Schaubühne* (1741–45), their collection of 'orderly' plays for the nation's theatre companies. Indeed, the Gottscheds were famously criticized by Lessing in the Seventeenth *Literaturbrief* for their slavish attachment to French culture and for failing to appreciate the English literary tradition. But the Gottscheds — and particularly Luise Gottsched — had a greater knowledge of and interest in English letters than is often acknowledged.

Luise Gottsched appears to have been curious about English and English literature from an early age. She was fortunate in having unusually good opportunities to learn the language and to immerse herself in English culture. She was first exposed to English in her childhood home in Danzig. Danzig in the early eighteenth century was a busy seaport and trade centre with a multilingual population. Gottsched's half-brother was taught English by one John Tompson — a British man residing in the city who later became the first Professor of English in Germany — and after his lessons he passed on to Gottsched what he had learnt from Tompson. In her early letters from Danzig to her future husband we find Gottsched quoting English literature and copying out a translation she had made of Joseph Addison's version of Psalm 23.[3] In this period she also tackled Addison's tragedy *Cato* (1713) — in the words of her husband many years later, 'zur Uebung im Englischen'.[4]

When Gottsched married Johann Christoph Gottsched in 1735 and moved to Leipzig, she would earn a reputation among her contemporaries for being the

2. Bernhard Fabian, 'English Books and their Eighteenth-Century German Readers', in *The Widening Circle: Essays on the Circulation of Literature in Eighteenth-Century Europe*, ed. by Paul J. Korshin (Philadelphia: University of Pennsylvania Press, 1976), pp. 119–96 (p. 126). See also Eva Maria Inbar, 'Zum Englischstudium im Deutschland des XVIII. Jahrhunderts', *Arcadia: Zeitschrift für vergleichende Literaturwissenschaft*, 15.1 (1980), 14–28.
3. Johann Christoph Gottsched, *Briefwechsel: Unter Einschluß des Briefwechsels von Luise Adelgunde Victorie Gottsched*, ed. by Detlef Döring and others, 25 vols (Berlin: de Gruyter, 2007–), III: *1734–1735* (2009), p. 245.
4. Johann Christoph Gottsched, 'Leben der weil. hochedelgebohrnen, nunmehr sel. Frau Luise Adelgunde Victoria Gottschedinn', in Luise Gottsched, *Sämmtliche kleinere Gedichte* (Leipzig: Breitkopf, 1763), n. p.

'englische Muse'.[5] She took on numerous translation projects from English. For instance, she rendered into German works on philosophy and religion by Anthony Ashley Cooper, 3rd Earl of Shaftesbury, George Berkeley and John Eachard; she helped to produce the first complete German edition of *The Spectator*, translating over half of the moral weekly's 635 issues; and she single-handedly tackled the whole of *The Guardian*.[6] She also seems to have been an energetic reviewer of English books for her husband's journal *Neuer Büchersaal der schönen Wissenschaften und freyen Künste*.[7]

In all this, she was supported by her husband's position in intellectual life and his extensive networks. Even in the book-fair town of Leipzig it was not always straightforward to lay one's hands on English-language publications but, by the end of her life, Gottsched had built up a sizable private library which included some 135 titles in English. Some of these books were sent to her directly from England or brought back from London for her by the couple's personal contacts.[8] Her collection would come to include a number of English grammars and dictionaries, among them John King's *Compleat English Guide for High-Germans*, James Greenwood's *Essay Towards a Practical English Grammar* and Samuel Johnson's *Dictionary of the English Language*.[9] In addition, it seems that Gottsched could draw sometimes on the expertise of native speakers: for instance, she apparently settled on the best translation of the title *The Guardian* after discussions with 'einiger gebohrnen Engländer und andrer Kenner dieser Sprache'.[10]

Gottsched appears to have had a special interest in Alexander Pope (1688–1744). Pope, whose literary career spanned most of the first half of the eighteenth century and whose output included poetry, prose pieces and translations, was

5. Marianne Wehr, 'Johann Christoph Gottscheds Briefwechsel: Ein Beitrag zur Geschichte der deutschen Frühaufklärung' (unpublished doctoral thesis, University of Leipzig, 1965), p. 111.
6. For more on the translations, see Brown, *Luise Gottsched the Translator*.
7. See Gabriele Ball, *Moralische Küsse: Gottsched als Zeitschriftenherausgeber und literarischer Vermittler* (Göttingen: Wallstein, 2000), pp. 194–200.
8. For instance, the English writer Charlotte Lennox sent Gottsched copies of her *Female Quixote* and *Shakespear Illustrated*; while Jacob Friedrich Lamprecht, one of Johann Christoph's disciples in Hamburg, brought a copy of Thomas Otway's domestic tragedy *The Orphan* back from London for her with the intention that she translate it. See Johann Christoph Gottsched, 'Catalogue de la Bibliotheque Choisie, de Feue Madame Gottsched, née Kulmus, proprement reliée en veau doré, et autres relieures Angloises, et Italiennes', in L. Gottsched, *Sämmtliche kleinere Gedichte*, pp. 487–532 (p. 512 and p. 514); Gustav Waniek, *Gottsched und die deutsche Litteratur seiner Zeit* (Leipzig: Breitkopf und Härtel, 1897; repr. Leipzig: Zentralantiquariat der DDR, 1972), p. 202.
9. See J. C. Gottsched, 'Catalogue de la Bibliotheque Choisie', p. 520, p. 523 and p. 525.
10. Luise Gottsched (trans.), *Der engländische Guardian oder Aufseher*, 2 vols (Leipzig: Breitkopf, 1749), n. p.

regarded in England as 'uncontestably the greatest poet of his age'.[11] It was *The Rape of the Lock* — first published in 1712 and expanded in 1714 — which helped to establish Pope as a writer. He subsequently turned his hand to a range of projects, including a translation of Homer's *Iliad* into heroic couplets, his mock-heroic satire on 'Dulness' *The Dunciad* (1728) and his philosophical poem aimed at vindicating the workings of God *An Essay on Man* (1733–34). Pope was only beginning to be discovered in Germany at the time when Gottsched started work on him: it appears that he first came to the attention of the German literati thanks to Voltaire's praise of him in the *Lettres philosophiques sur les Anglais* (1734).[12] In the late 1730s and 1740s he found a handful of readers such as the poets Barthold Hinrich Brockes and Friedrich von Hagedorn who saw much to admire in the neo-classical formality of his compositions: the tight metrical structures were seen as conveying clearly the matter of his poetry and representing a welcome break with baroque style. He would also come to be held in high regard for the positive, rationalist philosophy which seemed to underpin his work.

Gottsched returned to Pope again and again from the late 1730s onwards. She translated a number of pieces of short prose in the course of her work on the moral weeklies, such as a witty recipe for concocting an epic poem in *The Guardian* 78; she appears to have published a translation of his 'Universal Prayer' in the *Neuer Büchersaal* in 1750; she also believed she was translating Pope's 'Essay on the Life, Writings and Learning of Homer' for her *Neue Sammlung auserlesener Stücke aus Popens, Eachards, Newtons, und andrer Schriften* (1749) (the essay had appeared at the front of Pope's *Iliad* translation but had in fact been authored by Pope's collaborator Thomas Parnell). She also published reviews of a number of Pope-themed works, such as William Ayres's *Memoirs of the Life and Writings of Alexander Pope* and Johann Peter Uz's *Sieg des Liebesgottes: Eine Nachahmung des Popischen Lockenraubes.*

Her main work on Pope was her translation of *The Rape of the Lock*, a project which occupied her intermittently for many years. She may have been drawn to the poem in particular because its satirical nature. As part of their reforms of German culture, the Gottscheds and their circle were intent on promoting the merits of satire and fostering native literature written in this vein. They were aware that satirical writing was flourishing elsewhere in Enlightenment Europe and wanted to develop a similar tradition in Germany. In a sense, of course, satire fitted perfectly with the Enlightened notion that literature should be both

11. Thomas Woodman, 'Alexander Pope', in *Reader's Guide to Literature in English*, ed. by Mark Hawkins-Dady (London: Fitzroy Dearborn, 1996), pp. 605–07 (p. 605).
12. See Lawrence Marsden Price, *English Literature in Germany*, University of California Publications in Modern Philology, 37 (Berkeley: University of California Press, 1957), p. 61. See also Horst Oppel, *Englisch-deutsche Literaturbeziehungen*, Grundlagen der Anglistik und Amerikanistik, 1–2, 2 vols (Berlin: Schmidt, 1971), I, 62–64.

entertaining and instructive, for in making follies and depravities seem ridiculous, satire could improve the morals of society. It is striking that many of the texts which Gottsched translated over the course of her career can be termed satirical.[13]

The Rape of the Lock is a sparkling attack on the rituals and values of the English fashionable world. Pope was originally asked to compose the poem in order to put an end to a feud between two upper-class Catholic families, the Petres and the Fermors. The families, which had long been friendly, had become estranged on what seemed to be trifling grounds, the young Lord Petre having cut off a lock of Miss Arabella Fermor's hair. In the poem, Pope calls his lovers the 'Baron' and 'Belinda' and relates the incident in mock-heroic terms, which both emphasizes the families' unreasonable response to the event and allows the poet more generally to hold up to ridicule the confused values of his society. The poem describes a day in the life of the society belle: Belinda dresses for a game of cards as if arming herself for battle (Canto I); she sails down the Thames to Hampton Court with her guardian sylphs watching over her (Canto II); she enjoys victory at Ombre, as in an epic sports contest, but relinquishes a lock of her hair to the Baron (Canto III); she mourns the lock while the gnome Umbriel descends into the 'underworld' of the Cave of Spleen (Canto IV); and she engages in a battle-like skirmish with the Baron, attacking him with a hair-pin, but cannot find her lock because it has been transformed for posterity into a star (Canto V). Along the way, the poem comments wryly on wider social and political concerns such as attitudes to women, the relationship between the sexes, the government, and the legal system. This is a world where men are permitted to use 'fraud or force' to obtain women and no-one will bat an eyelid (II. 33–34), where statesmen spend as much time discussing romantic conquests as foreign policy (III. 5–6), where judges make hasty life-and-death decisions because they are eager to dine (III. 21–22).

Gottsched clearly expended a considerable amount of effort on the translation. *Der Lockenraub* was to be the first German translation of the poem in verse and the first to be made directly from English. As she explains in the preface, she began working on the translation in the late 1730s and was initially forced to use a French prose translation as her source text because she was unable to obtain a copy of the English original. Even at this point, it seems that she attempted to put the French translator's prose into verse. She managed to lay her hands on an English edition of *The Rape of the Lock* a few years later and claims to have been aghast at the difference between the French and English texts. She went back to the translation and revised it completely, retaining, she says, just five lines of her first version. The first edition of the translation was published in 1744 in a

13. See Hilary Brown, 'Luise Gottsched the Satirist', *Modern Language Review*, 103 (2008), 1036–50.

handsome volume complete with copperplate engravings by Anna Maria Werner, the court painter in Dresden.

Gottsched had not set herself an easy task. We do not know exactly what resources she had to hand while she was working on Pope: it is hard to imagine that she did not have recourse to an English dictionary but it is possible that she did not possess one of her own at this point.[14] In any case, there is much within the poem to challenge the translator. Pope's heroic couplets are compact, often carefully balanced, and linguistically playful. There are copious allusions to contemporary English life — certainly not always straightforward to decipher for someone who had never set foot in Britain. The poem is dense with imagery, and a range of motifs runs through the poem linked to ideas such as armour and warfare, cosmetics and clothing, beauty and fragility, and religious ritual. It is worth noting that there were other German translators who would not touch Pope with a bargepole. One critic writes of Johann Arnold Ebert, who in 1751 published a translation of Edward Young's *Night Thoughts*: 'It is undoubtedly no mere accident that Ebert, who enjoyed in his time the reputation of being the greatest German translator from the English, avoided Pope.'[15]

We should give credit to Gottsched for her achievement. She seems to be trying as far as possible to reproduce the distinctive features of the source text. In the first place, this means finding an equivalent verse form: Gottsched turns Pope's rhymed iambic pentameter into rhymed trochaic octameter with alternating masculine and feminine endings. In fact the metrical system is even more intricate than that: 'Within the octameter, a strict pattern is maintained: each line contains fifteen beats and is divided by a caesura into two equal hemistichs, one with a regular trochaic tetrameter, the other, a trochaic tetrameter catalectic. One couplet follows the basic movement, placing the catalectic hemistich after the caesura; in the next couplet, the sequence is inverted so that the catalectic tetrameter precedes the acatalectic.'[16] Gottsched often tries to mirror the rhythm of individual lines, for example by using the same or similar punctuation, as in 'Th'advent'rous Baron the bright locks admir'd, / He saw, he wish'd, and to the prize aspir'd' which Gottsched renders as 'Der verwegene *Baron*, den der Locken Reiz gefangen, / Sieht sie, wünscht sie, und wird kühn, dieses Kleinod zu erlangen'

14. The catalogue of Gottsched's library, published posthumously, lists two English dictionaries: Thomas Dyche and William Pardon, *A New General English Dictionary*, 4th edn (1744), which Gottsched may not have acquired before *Der Lockenraub* was published in 1744, and Samuel Johnson, A *Dictionary of the English Language*, 2nd edn (1756). See J. C. Gottsched, 'Catalogue de la Bibliotheque Choisie', p. 520.
15. J. H. Heinzelmann, 'Pope in Germany in the Eighteenth Century', *Modern Philology*, 10 (1913), 317–64.
16. Veronica C. Richel, 'Luise Gottsched's *Der Lockenraub* and Alexander Pope's *The Rape of the Lock*: A Comparative Analysis', *Neuphilologische Mitteilungen*, 3 (1975), 473–87 (p. 476).

(II. 29–30). In order to maintain the tight pattern of metre and rhyme, it is perhaps inevitable that she sometimes has to add an extra adjective or noun (e.g. II. 114, IV. 68, V. 42), or occasionally a phrase (e.g. III. 7, III. 30), or that she has to change the order of lines within a couplet or reorder the elements within a line (e.g. III. 134–35, V. 34). Ultimately, though, it is remarkable that her text usually corresponds line-by-line to Pope's and that she ends up with exactly the same number of couplets in each canto.

Despite the constraints of her verse form, many elements of the source text are indeed conveyed in German.[17] Granted, she seems to struggle with the odd line, particularly those containing culture-specific references, which she appears at times to have misconstrued. For example, in Pope's poem, lovers in bed until noon call their servants by ringing handbells and tapping their slippers on the floor: 'Thrice rung the bell, the slipper knock'd the ground'; Gottsched translates this as 'Dreymal tönete die Glocke; der Pantoffel wird bewegt' (I. 17) and adds a note stating 'Vermuthlich ist es in London, wie an vielen andern Orten gewöhnlich, daß um eilf Uhr eine große Bethglocke dreymal angeschlagen wird.' She also tends to leave out or tone down phrases with sexual overtones, perhaps conscious of social mores. For instance, while Pope's Belinda cries out 'Oh hadst thou, cruel! been content to seize / Hairs less in sight, or any hairs but these!' (IV. 175–76), Gottsched's Belinde avoids any hint of innuendo: 'Grausamer! erschrickst du nicht, daß du, wider dein Gewissen, / Dieses Kleinod meinem Haupt mit verruchter Faust entrissen?'. But elsewhere Gottsched comes up with good solutions for culture-specific references, finding alternatives more familiar to her German readers (e.g. in her substitution of the card game 'Scherwenzel' for 'Lu' in Canto III) or adding an explanatory footnote (e.g. V. 136). She has gathered that an '*Indian* screen' stood in front of the fire (III. 14; 'Feuerschirm') and that 'Angels in machines' are props in the Augustan theatre (IV. 46; 'Engel aus der Opernwelt'). And she manages to pack into her octameters much of Pope's vivid imagery and biting humour. For example, the following passage, taken from Canto I, describes Belinda at her dressing-table:

> And now, unveil'd, the Toilet stands display'd,
> Each silver Vase in mystic order laid.
> First, robe'd in white, the nymph intent adores
> With head uncover'd, the Cosmetic pow'rs.
> A heav'nly Image in the glass appears,
> To that she bends, to that her eyes she rears;
> Th' inferior Priestess, at her altar's side,

17. Richel reaches a similar conclusion in her analysis of the translation, calling *Der Lockenraub* 'the most noteworthy [of Gottsched's translations of belles-lettres]' and 'a most admirable performance.' Richel, 'Luise Gottsched's *Der Lockenraub*', p. 474 and p. 487. See also Veronica C. Richel, *Luise Gottsched: A Reconsideration* (Bern: Peter Lang, 1973), pp. 72–84.

Trembling, begins the sacred rites of Pride.
Unnumber'd treasures ope at once, and here
The various off'rings of the world appear;
From each she nicely culls with curious toil,
And decks the Goddess with the glitt'ring spoil.
This casket India's glowing gems unlocks,
And all Arabia breathes from yonder box.
The Tortoise here and Elephant unite,
Transform'd to combs, the speckled, and the white.
Here files of pins extend their shining rows,
Puffs, Powders, Patches, Bibles, Billet-doux. (I. 121–38)

Jetzt bemerkt man, daß ihr Fuß zum enthüllten Nachttisch gehet,
Wo manch silbernes Gefäß in verborgner Ordnung stehet.
Sie verehrt, mit bloßem Haupte, und in einer weißen Tracht,
Das kosmetische Vermögen, das die Schönheit reizend macht.
Sie erblickt ein himmlisch Bild, das auf hellem Glase schwebet,
Und zu dem sich ehrfurchtsvoll ihrer Augen Stral erhebet.
Eine mindre Opferschwester macht sich, mit gebognem Knie,
Zitternd zu des Altars Seiten, an des Putzwerks Liturgie.
Hundert Schachteln öffnen sich, mit den ungezählten Schätzen
Aller Opfer der Natur, die der Menschen Stolz ergetzen.
Fast aus jeder wird mit Sorgfalt etwas glänzendes geklaubt;
Und der Raub des ganzen Erdballs decket nun der Göttinn Haupt.
Indiens geschliffnen Kies sieht man häufig hier erscheinen,
Ganz Arabien dampft auch, mitten unter Edelsteinen.
Das Gehäuse großer Kröten, und der Elephantenzahn,
Haben sich allhier als Kämme, bunt und weiß, hervorgethan.
Dichtgesteckter Nadeln Heer strahlt in reinen Silberflammen;
Puder, Schönfleck, Liebesbrief, Bibel, alles liegt beysammen!

Pope is clearly mocking Belinda's vanity here: the heroine practises self-worship with the seriousness of a religious ritual, and the scene is presented in mock-religious (indeed blasphemous) terms. Gottsched manages to sustain the imagery throughout the passage: 'a heav'nly Image' ('ein himmlisch Bild), 'her altar's side' ('des Altars Seiten'), 'sacred rites of Pride' ('des Putzwerks Liturgie'). At the same time, the poet underlines Belinda's obsession with outer appearance by weaving in mock-heroic language. These images, too, are carried across in German. Instead of armour, it is jewellery and perfume which form 'the glitt'ring spoil' ('der Raub des ganzen Erdballs'); instead of soldiers, it is 'files of pins' ('Dichtgesteckter Nadeln Heer') which line up to serve the goddess. And the sting of course comes in the last line when Pope suggests that Belinda cannot distinguish between the value of a powder-puff and that of a Bible — a list captured in Gottsched's translation too.

Der Lockenraub broke new ground with respect to the reception of Pope in Germany. True, Pope was beginning to find admiring readers in the late 1730s and 1740s. In Hamburg, Brockes published a translation of the *Essay on Man* in 1740 and Hagedorn a translation of the 'Universal Prayer' in 1742; there also seem to be echoes of Pope in the work of both poets in this decade. But, beyond a handful of literati, Pope would not have been widely known and Gottsched's edition of *Der Lockenraub* would have helped to draw attention to the English writer.

Der Lockenraub can also be considered a significant achievement because it represents an attempt to bring new impulses into literary discourse in mid-eighteenth-century Germany and to further the Gottscheds' cultural political agenda. It becomes clear from the way that Gottsched presents the target text that she is making a conscious effort to challenge the dominance of French culture. The translation is framed by paratextual material — the preface, footnotes, an appendix — which together amount to a fairly vitriolic attack on the French. While this may surprise us initially, given the Gottscheds' reputation as Francophiles, it is typical of the couple's actually rather ambivalent attitude towards France. Their admiration and emulation of certain aspects of French life and letters stemmed from a desire to promote German culture and was tempered throughout their careers with an awareness that France's strength — political as well as cultural and intellectual — was a challenge to the burgeoning self-confidence of their own nation. As far as literature was concerned, for instance, they were engaged around the time that Gottsched was working on *The Rape of the Lock* in efforts to counter Eléazar de Mauvillon's attack on the Germans in his *Lettres françaises et germaniques, ou Réflexions militaires, litteraires et critiques sur les François et les Allemands* (1740). Mauvillon, a French Huguenot who was Private Secretary to the Prince-Elector of Saxony and later taught French at the University of Leipzig, had written depreciatingly of the German language and German literature in his *Lettres*, in particular repeating the old claim that, in contrast to the French, the Germans could not produce great literature because of their lack of 'esprit'.[18] Mauvillon's work was seized on by the Swiss critics Johann Jakob Bodmer and Johann Jacob Breitinger in their attempt to discredit the Gottsched school in the early 1740s, provoking defensive and occasionally aggressively anti-French responses in Leipzig. Through her translation, then, it is as if Gottsched is hoping to open up new perspectives for German literature by familiarizing readers with a writer from a different country and, more generally, to free her compatriots from their veneration of all things French.

On one level, Gottsched's criticism in the paratexts is directed at current literary practices in France, specifically in the field of translation. She reproves

18. See Roland Krebs, '*Les Lettres françaises et germaniques* de Mauvillon et leur réception en Allemagne', *Dix-Huitième Siècle*, 14 (1982), 377–90. See also Roland Krebs, 'La France jugée par Gottsched: ennemie héréditaire ou modèle culturel?', *Revue d'Allemagne*, 18 (1986), 585–99.

repeatedly the French translator whose edition she had been forced to use before she had access to the text in English and which she later found to deviate so drastically from Pope's text despite the translator claiming to follow Pope to the letter. She vents her fury in the preface at his unfaithful approach and at the French habit of producing *belles infidèles*, translations which played fast and loose with any notions of literalness. In the main text, she incorporates many footnotes pointing to sections of the poem which were distorted in the French version. She also includes an appendix containing two of her own 'free' translations of poems by Antoinette du Ligier de la Garde Deshoulières as an act of revenge ('Man muß doch den Herren Franzosen einmal zeigen, wie es einem Schriftsteller gefällt, wenn man nach eigner Willkür mit ihm umgeht').[19] She undoubtedly chose her target carefully: Deshoulières had been the most highly regarded lyric poet in France in the late seventeenth century. There is a sense in which Gottsched's exasperation is rhetorical — as she herself says, she was well aware of the French *belles infidèles* translation tradition before she sat down with the French version of Pope — and serves primarily as an opportunity to throw up her hands in horror at the presumptuousness of French littérateurs.

Gottsched broadens her criticism too and lambastes the French nation more generally. She uses nearly four pages of the preface to respond to an article which had appeared the previous year in the *Journal littéraire d'Allemagne*, a publication established by French Huguenots who had fled to Germany and now wanted to introduce German letters to a French-speaking public. In the article in question, Gottsched had been taken to task for being too negative about the French in the preface to her *Zwo Schriften, das Maaß der lebendigen Kräfte betreffend* (1741), her translation of work by the French scientists Emilie du Châtelet and Jean-Jacque Dortous de Mairan. There Gottsched had praised Châtelet for her support of the German scholar Leibniz over Descartes and Newton in a long-standing scientific debate about the force of bodies in motion, taking it as evidence that Germany could now boast great minds who were challenging the dominance of the French in the republic of letters. In the preface to *Der Lockenraub*, Gottsched defends her view that France is no longer bringing forth as many intellectual luminaries as in the past. For example, she pours scorn on Pierre-Louis Moreau de Maupertuis, the French scientist who had led an expedition to the Arctic Circle which had seemed merely to confirm the theories of his seventeenth-century forerunners. She is scornful, too, of Voltaire, for writing a bad epigram ('[einem] sehr schlechten Sinngedichte') about Maupertuis. She suggests that this disproves

19. The source texts appear to have been 'Epitre Chagrine à Mademoiselle de la Charce (1685)' and 'Epitre Chagrine à Mademoiselle ****'. For further discussion of these translations, see Katherine R. Goodman, *Amazons and Apprentices: Women and the German Parnassus in the Early Enlightenment* (Rochester, NY: Camden House, 1999), pp. 233–44.

proclamations by arrogant Frenchmen such as Mauvillon — or the abbé Bouhours, who had famously expressed a similar view to Mauvillon some decades earlier and whom Gottsched mentions here — about the superiority of French over German literature. Gottsched weaves a string of names and references into this section of the preface, and presumably any of her contemporaries with an interest in current European affairs would have been able to appreciate the polemic.

In general, it appears that *Der Lockenraub* was well received. It was discussed at length in several journals: reviewers compared the translation to Pope's original text, praised the translator for her efforts, and quoted striking excerpts. Such comments are typical:

> An einer guten deutschen Dollmetschung hat es bishieher gefehlet: in der Thataber gehört Pope nicht unter die Schriftsteller, welche sich leicht übersetzen lassen. Seine Fähigkeit viel Gedancken in wenig Worte zusammenzubringen, seine ausgesuchten englischen Redensarten, und die besondere Art solche zu verbinden, machen dem der dessen Verse in eine andere Sprache bringen will, nicht wenig zu schaffen. Es ist nicht allen gelungen, welche sich daran gewaget: Und wir entsinnen uns wohl ehe eine Ubersetzung eines seiner poetischen Schriften gelesen zu haben, die wir nicht zu verstehen vermocht, wo wir nicht den Grundtext zu Hülffe genommen. Es ist also eine in der That schwere Beschäftigung, so die Frau Professor Gottschedin unternommen, Popens Lockenraub nicht allein deutsch zu machen, sondern denselben so gar in deutsche Verse zu übersetzen: aber es bringt derselben auch desto grössern Ruhm, da sie solches glücklich hinaus geführet. Wir haben das Deutsche sorgfältig gegen das Englische gehalten, und befunden, daß sie theils Popens Sinn getreulich ausgedrucket, theils aber ihren Vortrag so deutlich und angenehm gemacht, daß diejenigen welche solchen nach den Grundsätzen der deutschen Sprachkunst beurtheilen, damit zufrieden seyn werden.[20]

The translation seems to have made an impact on the literary world. Pope became very popular as a model for German poets from the 1750s onwards and remained an important source of inspiration throughout the second half of the century. As Horst Oppel remarks: 'Vor allem setzte *The Rape of the Lock* den einmal begonnenen Siegeszug fort'.[21]

In particular, it appears that *Der Lockenraub* provided a model for mock-heroic poetry, which the Gottscheds were particularly keen to promote because of its satirical bent. The form was not entirely unknown: there were earlier examples of the genre such as Tassoni's *La secchia rapita* (1622) and Boileau's *Le Lutrin*

20. *Zuverläßige Nachrichten von dem gegenwärtigen Zustande, Veränderung und Wachsthum der Wissenschaften*, 63 (1745), 219–28. See also *Bemühungen zur Beförderung der Critik und des guten Geschmacks*, 1.7 (1744), 562–66 and *Göttingische Zeitung von gelehrten Sachen*, 6 (1744), 531–32.
21. Oppel, *Englisch-deutsche Literaturbeziehungen*, I, 64.

(1674). But in the mid-eighteenth century, we find renewed efforts to encourage this type of writing. Both Gottscheds were interested in the mock heroic: Johann Christoph included his translation of part of *Le Lutrin* in the proceedings of the Leipzig literary society, the Deutsche Gesellschaft, and published his own mock-heroic poems *Der Proceß* (1740) and *Der Dichterkrieg* (1741–42) in the years when Gottsched was working on her *Rape of the Lock* translation.[22] As noted above, Gottsched must surely have been drawn to *The Rape of the Lock* in part because it fell under the heading of satire. The satire was of course directed not just at the Petres and Fermors or the English *beau monde*; the poem can be read as a much broader critique of the muddled values which could lie at the heart of any modern society. It is interesting that the translation is presented to the reader with the suggestion that the satire could be applied just as well to Germany as to Britain. For one thing, Gottsched is not consistent in the way she translates references to contemporary English life: Belinde may sail down the 'Themse' (II. 4) to 'Hampton' (III. 4), but a moment in her card game is compared to 'Scherwenzel' (III. 62) rather than 'Lu' (the former being a game played in Germany in the eighteenth century) and one of the handmaids in the Cave of Spleen holds in her hands Michael Cubach's *Großes Gebet-Buch*, a German prayer-book popular at the time. Furthermore, the copperplate engravings by Anna Maria Werner which adorn the text do not specifically depict contemporary London, and in fact the plate which accompanies Canto III is clearly based on a Leipzig coffee-house.[23] In the years after the publication of Gottsched's translation, we find many mock-heroic poems being written in Germany, including many which were heavily indebted to *The Rape of the Lock*.[24] When Gottsched reviewed Uz's *Sieg des Liebesgottes* for *Das Neueste aus der anmuthigen Gelehrsamkeit* in 1753, she was gratified to see that her fellow Germans were now proving they could reach the same heights as Pope:

> Wir haben in langer Zeit kein so angenehmes und artiges Scherzgedicht gesehen; ja wir können sagen, daß es in der Art spaßhafter Epopöen, dasjenige sey, welches dem Lockenraube am nächsten kömmt. Wir sehen mit Vergnügen, daß der deutsche Witz, auch den feinen Scherz, und die leichtfertige Satire, mit einer richtigen Art zu denken, und regelmäßigen Art zu dichten, verbinden kann. Denn hier verbindet sich alles: schöne Gedanken, neue Bilder, ein starker Ausdruck, wohlgewählte Beywörter, und doch eine fehlerfreye Schreibart, und ein reines Sylbenmaaß.[25]

22. Cf. Waniek, pp. 429–30.
23. Eleonora Höschele, 'Von "gunst zur wahrheit angetrieben": Leben und Werk der Dresdner Hofzeichnerin Anna Maria Werner', *Jahrbuch der Staatlichen Kunstsammlungen Dresden*, 28 (2000), 33–46 (p. 41).
24. See Erich Petzet, 'Die deutschen Nachahmungen des Popeschen *Lockenraubes*', *Zeitschrift für vergleichende Literaturgeschichte*, 4 (1891), 409–33.
25. *Das Neueste aus der anmuthigen Gelehrsamkeit*, 3 (1753), 239–40 (239).

Engraving by Anna Maria Werner for Canto III for the first edition of Gottsched's translation. Luise Gottsched (trans.), *Herrn Alexander Popens Lockenraub: Ein scherzhaftes Heldengedicht* (Leipzig: Breitkopf, 1744). Universitätsbibliothek Leipzig, 95-8-1819, Stich Nr. 3

Gottsched may have carried on reworking her *Rape of the Lock* translation in private. In 1772, nearly three decades after the publication of *Der Lockenraub* and some years after the deaths of both Gottscheds, a second, revised edition of the text appeared. The edition was published by the Leipzig company Breitkopf who had issued the original version and who had been the Gottscheds' main publisher over the years. It includes a new four-page preface outlining the circumstances which had given rise to the second edition; interestingly, there is no indication of who has written the preface. The writer claims that the revisions were undertaken by Gottsched herself. According to him/her, Gottsched had taken to heart a critical review of *Der Lockenraub* which had appeared in the *Freymüthige Nachrichten von neuen Büchern, und andern zur Gelehrtheit gehörigen Sachen* in 1744, a Zurich literary journal associated with the Gottscheds' adversary Bodmer. She decided to go back to the translation and correct the errors highlighted by the reviewer as well as rework the text as a whole: 'Sie erkannte, daß an ihrer Arbeit noch verschiedenes zu verbessern, und sie nicht immer genugsam auf ihrer Hut gewesen wäre. Es fielen ihr noch andere Flecken in die Augen, als diejenigen, welche man getadelt hatte. Sie nahm sich also vor, dieselben sorgfältig ab zu wischen, so viel es sich thun ließe.'[26] The writer of the preface claims that Gottsched did not see fit to issue a second edition of *Der Lockenraub* during her lifetime due to the ill repute into which the Leipzig school had fallen; the timing was now right because people were starting to look more favourably on the Gottscheds, as evidenced by the positive reception of Dorothea von Runckel's recent edition of Luise Gottsched's letters (1771–72).

It may not be possible to ascertain whether the second edition really was the work of Gottsched. We know that Gottsched was fascinated by Pope, and by *The Rape of the Lock* in particular, and had been prepared to revise her translation once before. It is conceivable that she withheld it from publication because she did not want to give the Swiss critics the satisfaction of seeing that she agreed with them in some respects. But there is no mention of ongoing work on *Der Lockenraub* either in Johann Christoph's detailed biography of his wife or in any of her letters which have been published thus far.[27] It is not beyond the bounds of possibility that the second edition was the work of a later translator wanting to capitalize on the marketing potential of the Gottsched name.

26. *Herrn Alexander Popens Lockenraub: Ein scherzhaftes Heldengedicht. Aus dem Englischen in deutsche Verse übersetzet von Luisen Adelgunden Victorien Gottschedinn. In dieser zweyten Auflage durchaus verbessert, und beynahe ganz umgearbeitet* (Leipzig: Breitkopf, 1772), p. xvii.

27. J. C. Gottsched, 'Leben'; Luise Gottsched, *Briefe*, ed. by Dorothea von Runckel, 3 vols (Dresden: Harpeter, 1771–72). It is possible that future volumes of the Gottscheds' correspondence will bring to light new material relating to the translation: J. C. Gottsched, *Briefwechsel: Unter Einschluß des Briefwechsels von Luise Adelgunde Victorie Gottsched.* At the time of writing the first seven volumes have appeared, covering the years 1722–41.

In any case, the overall tendency of the second edition was to make the translation even more closely oriented to the source text. The verse form remains rhymed trochaic octameter but many of the lines themselves are rephrased. The author of the review in the *Freymüthige Nachrichten von neuen Büchern* had listed a number of examples from the first edition where the translator had not captured the full sense or poetry of Pope's original: for example, (s)he had picked out lines where Gottsched had omitted or toned down sexual innuendos and had criticized her for less vivid word choices: 'Sie giebt *Spright*, *Genius*, *Dæmon*, durch das einzige *Poltergeist* und *Termagent* heißt bey ihr ebenfalls ein *Poltergeist*'.[28] These types of choices are now revisited. Pope's most graphic lines are rendered more faithfully — as in 'Oh hadst thou, cruel! been content to seize / Hairs less in sight, or any hairs but these!' which becomes 'Hättest du, Grausamer, doch dich begnügt, solch Haar zu fassen, / Das nicht so vor Augen liegt, und nur dieses da gelassen!' (IV. 175–76) — and the text is not populated with so many poltergeister: '*Fays, Fairies, Genii, Elves* and *Dæmons* hear!' is no longer translated as '*Hexen, Zaubrer, Poltergeist, Alp*, und was ich herbeschieden' but '*Feyen, Nickse, Genii, Dämones* und *Aelfen* höret' (II. 74). In many respects, the aim stated in the new preface seems to have been achieved: 'Sie nahm sich also vor [...] dieß Gedicht dem Sinne seines Verfassers gemäßer zu machen, damit Pope auch im Deutschen, wenn es angienge, noch immer Pope bleibe.'[29]

However, even the first *Lockenraub* had been an impressive achievement. It had brought German readers into contact with a major English writer at a time when English literature was only beginning to be discovered in Germany. The translation shows that the Gottscheds' programme for reforming German culture was more cosmopolitan and avant-garde than is often recognized: it involved looking beyond France to other European literary traditions and drawing on appropriate models wherever they were to be found, regardless of language. Gottsched braved the challenges of Pope and, in doing so, made an important contribution to efforts to establish a national literary canon in eighteenth-century Germany.

28. *Freymüthige Nachrichten von neuen Büchern, und andern zur Gelehrtheit gehörigen Sachen*, 1 (1744), 278–80 and 283–86 (p. 285).
29. *Herrn Alexander Popens Lockenraub*, p. xvii.

Engraving by Anna Maria Werner for Canto I for the first edition of Gottsched's translation. Luise Gottsched (trans.), *Herrn Alexander Popens Lockenraub: Ein scherzhaftes Heldengedicht* (Leipzig: Breitkopf, 1744). Universitätsbibliothek Leipzig, 95-8-1819, Stich Nr. 1.

Vorrede.

Mein Leser,

Ich überliefere dir hiermit die Uebersetzung eines der scharfsinnigsten Werke des berühmten *Pope*, welches allenthalben so bald Leser und Beyfall gefunden, als es die Presse verlassen gehabt: daher mir es wohl niemand verargen wird, daß ich mich mit dieser Arbeit beschäfftiget. Es sind bereits 6 bis 7 Jahre verflossen, daß ich, theils aus eigener Bewegniß, theils auf Anrathen guter Freunde, dieselbe angefangen: dennoch arbeitete ich nur furchtsam daran, indem ich kein ander Original hatte, als die französische ungebundene Uebersetzung, welche zu Paris 1728 in 12, von einem Ungenannten herausgegeben worden. Ich wußte nämlich schon damals, was mich nach diesem eine beständige Erfahrung täglich mehr gelehret hat, daß nichts ungetreuers und abweichenders zu finden sey, als die Uebersetzungen der Franzosen. Es sey nun, daß eine gewisse natürliche Leichtsinnigkeit dieses Volks, oder ein inneres hochmüthiges Vorurtheil, nach welchem es denket, ein Schriftsteller müsse sich nothwendig unter seinen Händen verschönern, es möge auch mit ihm machen, was es wolle, hieran schuld sey: so ist es doch gewiß, daß ein jeder, der nur eine französische Uebersetzung auf die Probe stellen will, dieses erfahren wird. Ich bemühete mich also, den Grundtext aus England zu bekommen; aber einige Jahre vergebens. Einige Freunde, denen ich das erste Buch vorlas, ermunterten mich, meine Arbeit fortzusetzen, und mich genau an den französischen Text zu halten, weil man doch nichts mehr von mir fordern könnte, als was ich vor Augen hätte. Hierzu kam noch, daß jemand in Dresden mit einer prosaischen deutschen Uebersetzung dieses Gedichts ans Licht trat, die er, wie er auf dem Titel angab, aus dem Englischen gemacht haben wollte; die aber in der That von Wort zu Worte meine französische Uebersetzung mit allen ihren Fehlern war. Da ich nun gleich anfangs meine Uebersetzung in Versen gemacht hatte, um einige sehr matte und schläfrige Stellen in der französischen Dollmetschung ein wenig kürzer und lebhafter zu geben: so ermunterte man mich abermals, mein poetisches Kleid für den *popischen Lockenraub* fertig zu machen. Ich that es auch endlich, und war bereits mit den 4 ersten Büchern fertig, als ich das englische Original in die Hände bekam. Ich setzte mich begierig nieder, um sowohl mich, als meinen gallischen Dollmetscher, mit *Popen* zu vergleichen. Aber wie erstaunte ich nicht! und wie sehr reuete mich meine Zeit und Mühe, als ich sah, wie weit wir von dieses großen Dichters Feuer, Scharfsinnigkeit, kurzen nachdrücklichen Satiren, und edlen poetischen Beschreibungen, entfernet waren.

Das war nichts minder, als *Popens Lockenraub*! und man muß ein Franzose seyn, das heißt, den Schutz aller Vorurtheile der Deutschen, von der Vortrefflichkeit dieses Volks, genießen, um mit einer solchen Arbeit nicht ausgezischet zu werden. Und gleichwohl hat er das Herz gehabt, in der Vorrede zu sagen: *seine Uebersetzung folge genau dem Buchstaben; er habe nichts abgekürzt noch hinzugesetzt, und wenn er ja abwiche, so geschähe es nur in Kleinigkeiten.*[1] Wahrlich! eine Kühnheit, die viel mehrere solche Lügenbestrafungen verdienet hätte, als ich einige wenige unter meinen Text gesetzt: denn sonst würde mein Werk, mehr Noten als Grundtext bekommen, und gar zu gelehrt ausgesehen haben. Ich war also über meiner verlornen Zeit, und einer Arbeit, die mir doch bereits viele Mühe gemacht hatte, ja über meinen französischen Verführer, so verdrießlich; daß ich alles voller Unmuth hinwarf, mit dem Vorsatze, allen Uebersetzungen, nach französischen Dollmetschern, gänzlich zu entsagen. Welchen Rath ich auch allen denen geben will, die ihre Zeit und Mühe nicht verlieren wollen.

Vielleicht wird hier mein Eifer, gegen den gewissenlosen *französischen Uebersetzer des Lockenraubes*, so klein er auch ist, einigen Herren wieder zu stark vorkommen, die, ob sie gleich unter deutschem Schutze stehen, den ihnen ihr Vaterland versaget, und in deutschen Diensten sind, dennoch eine Ehre darinnen suchen, Frankreich groß zu machen, und alle andre Völker dagegen zu verkleinern. Man wundert[2] sich nämlich gar sehr, daß die Deutschen einmal anfangen, die so lange vergrößerte und von uns blindlings geglaubte Größe der französischen Verdienste zu untersuchen, und es frey herauszusagen: man fände, daß sie auch schwache Menschen sind, und es habe unserm Vaterlande an großen Männern niemals gefehlet, fehle ihm auch voritzo nicht an solchen, die es mit allen gallischen Sternen erster Größe gar wohl aufnehmen, und selbige gar verdunkeln können. Das ist nun freylich ein verwägner Eingriff in den bisherigen ruhigen Besitz des französischen Vorzuges vor den Deutschen! Und was das ärgste ist, so bin ich die arme Sünderinn, die sich in einem Schreiben an die *Marquisinn von Chatelet*[3] so gröblich vergangen hat. Man kann es nicht vergessen, daß ich daselbst zu der *Frau von Chatelet* gesaget habe:

> Dein Land, das Vaterland, so vieler großen Geister,
> Zählt jetzt nur einzelne, und doch nur halbe Meister.

Man bringt auch so gar endlich drey Männer auf, welche in Frankreich bekannt zu werden anfangen, und allen ehemaligen berühmten Franzosen, die Wage halten sollen. Ich habe alle Hochachtung gegen dieselben, allein ich glaube auch,

1. 'Elle (la Traduction) est très litterale. On n'a rien retranché ni ajouté; et si elle renferme quelques differences, elles sont très legères.'
2. Siehe das *Journal litteraire d'Allemagne &c.* Tom. II. Part. 2. aufs 1743 Jahr, auf der 420. und 421. Seite.
3. Es steht vor der Uebersetzung zwoer Schriften, das Maaß der lebendigen Kräfte betreffend.

daß sich keiner von ihnen mit einem *Cartesius*, *Malebransche*, *Rohault*, *Gassendi*, *Regis* und *Pascal* vergleichen wird. Sollte z. E. wohl Herr *Maupertuis* seine geringe Bemühung im Norden mit der Arbeit eines *Piccards* und *Caßini* in Vergleichung setzen, die durch ganz Frankreich eine Mittagslinie ausgemessen? Zwar hat Herr *Maupertuis* mehr gefroren, als jene, welches für einen Mann aus seinem Lande schon sehr viel ist: aber übrigens hat er auch nichts mehr gethan, als daß er das, was *Huygen* und *Newton* lange vorher gelehrt, wahr befunden hat. Ja ich zweifele nicht, daß es noch zehn Männer in Frankreich giebt, die auf königliche Kosten, und unter dem Schutze ihres Landesherren, diese Arbeit eben auch ganz gut würden verrichtet, und sich deswegen noch nicht für die Ehre dieser Welt haben schelten lassen: wie Herr *Voltaire* den Hrn. *Maupertuis* in einem sehr schlechten Sinngedichte nennet; womit Pater *Bouhours* gar nicht zufrieden seyn würde. Ich hoffe, daß ich mich auf diesen französischen Kunstrichter um so viel unparteyischer werde berufen können, da es eben derselbe ist, der die saubere Frage aufgeworfen: 'si un Allemand peut avoir de l'esprit?' und ohne daß er von deutscher Seite, etwa durch eine Frage: 'si un François peut avoir le sens commun?' dazu wäre veranlasset worden.

Uebrigens bedaure ich die Mühe, die man sich in Uebersetzung des Wortes *Afterbrut* gegeben, da man 'posterité' dafür gesetzt, welches aber meinen Sinn gar nicht ausdrückt. Ich bin nämlich gar nicht in Abrede, daß ich unter *Afterbrut* eine *Misgeburt*, oder eine aus der Art geschlagene Zucht verstehe: und mein Gegner selbst würde meiner Meynung seyn, wenn er meine Worte noch einmal hätte überlesen wollen. Ich sage:

> Ganz Deutschland denkt, wie ich, seit eine Afterbrut
> Auf Frankreichs alten Ruhm, recht keck und trotzig thut;
> Und, da nicht Witz, nicht Recht, das kalte Blatt begeistert,
> Sich selbst zum Midas setzt, und bessre Völker meistert.
> Man spricht uns Witz, und Kunst, Verstand, und Tugend ab,
> Man bricht uns ungekannt, und ungehört den Stab:
> Als würd ein ganzes Land, sich einst nach Köpfen richten,
> Die ihrer Väter Ruhm, durch eignen Schimpf, zernichten.

Ich hoffe doch nicht, daß mein Gegner sich solcher Leute annehmen wird, die so unbillig mit uns verfahren; und daß er sich ihnen zu Liebe die Mühe nehmen wird, auf eine gelinde Uebersetzung des wohlverdienten Namens, *Afterbrut* zu sinnen. Allein es kömmt mir fast so vor, als dächte er, ich hätte die *ganze* französische Nation gemeynt; da ich doch nur diejenigen meyne, die sich an uns so gröblich vergehen. Verhoffentlich aber wird er deren Partey nicht nehmen, und wenn es auch der Herr *d'Argens* selbst seyn sollte; der so lange auf die Deutschen lästert, bis ihm einmal ein patriotisch gesinnter guter Kopf zeigen wird, daß die Satire auch in Deutschland zu Hause sey.

Ich hätte freylich, wie mein Herr Gegner gar wohl anmerkt, die *Frau von Chatelet* loben können, ohne auf einige von ihren Landesleuten zu schimpfen.

Ich sehe es gar wohl ein, daß diese Freyheit völlig in meiner Macht gestanden hätte. Allein wenn nur die billigern Franzosen anfangen werden, den Deutschen Recht zu schaffen, und ihren Mitbrüdern die Unbilligkeit zu verweisen, die man gegen die Deutschen bisher bewiesen hat, und noch täglich beweiset; so wird man diese Gnugthuung für hinlänglich halten. Vielleicht aber wird man dieses noch ferner vergeblich hoffen. Und in diesem Falle wird man es den Deutschen nicht übel nehmen können, wenn sie sich selbst Recht schaffen. Ich habe auch in meinem Schreiben an die *Frau von Chatelet* nur gesagt, daß Frankreich vormals größere Männer aufzuweisen gehabt hätte, als itzo: und mich dünkt, ein unparteyischer Richter müßte in der gelehrten Welt sehr unerfahren seyn, wenn er hieran zweifeln wollte. Haben wir es nicht noch kürzlich gesehen, daß Frankreich keinen *Fleschier* mehr hat?

Wiewohl ich bescheide mich gern, daß das Lob, welches ich der *Frau von Chatelet* gegeben, sich, so wie damals, also auch noch jetzt, bloß darauf gründet, daß sie wirklich so grundgelehrt sey, als ich und viele andere sie gehalten; und daß ich allerdings ganz anders würde haben reden müssen, wenn dasjenige wahr wäre, was ein gewisser *Schweizer*, seit einiger Zeit ausgebreitet hat.

Ich glaube über dieses nicht zu irren, wenn ich dafür halte, daß nicht mein poetisches Schreiben, meinen Gegner aufgebracht; sondern ein gewisser Ausdruck, dessen ich mich in der Vorrede bedienet habe, und davon man nur sagt: 'le trait est un peu vif'. Dieses Urtheil ist so bescheiden und höflich, daß es mich ganz entwaffnet. Ist mein Gegner mit dem Bekenntnisse zufrieden, daß mein Ausdruck mir selbst so vorkömmt, und daß es mir leid ist, einen Mann beleidiget zu haben, der mit seinen Gegnern so glimpflich verfähret, oder verfahren läßt: so wird es mir sehr angenehm seyn, und ich versichere ihn meiner Hochachtung.

Ich komme wieder auf die Nachricht von meiner Uebersetzung. Ich hatte sie eine geraume Zeit in ihrer ersten Gestalt liegen lassen, als eine Gelegenheit vorfiel, daß ich sie einer gewissen jungen Gräfinn, die so wie an Schönheit, also auch an Einsicht in die schönen Wissenschaften, es den allermeisten ihres Geschlechts und Standes zuvor thut, vor Augen bringen sollte. Ich schämte mich, ihr ein Werk zu zeigen, welches unvollständig war, und übersetzte also das fünfte Buch nach dem englischen Originale. Diese Arbeit gieng mir leichter und glücklicher von statten, als ich anfangs geglaubet hatte. Das nach dem Grundtexte übersetzte Buch klang auch viel edler und körnichter, als meine vorige Uebersetzung, und ungeachtet ich es damals nur bey diesem letzten Buche bewenden ließ, und das ganze Werk, so wie es war, in obgedachte Hände lieferte, bey denen es auch noch jetzo liegt: so entschloß ich mich doch, mit der Zeit auch die vier ersten Bücher nach dem Grundtexte umzuarbeiten. Diese Umarbeitung aber mußte eine ganz neue Uebersetzung werden, indem ich von aller meiner ersten Arbeit nur fünf Zeilen habe brauchen können: so genau ich auch bey meinem französischen Texte geblieben.

Und in diesem neuen Zustande überliefere ich dir, *mein Leser*, gegenwärtigen *Lockenraub*. Ich habe mir dabey so viel Mühe gegeben, daß mir die Lust zu mehrern solchen Ubersetzungen ziemlich vergangen ist. Ungeachtet nun eine Uebersetzung nicht für diejenigen gemacht zu seyn scheint, die die Grundsprache verstehen: so könnte es doch kommen, daß gewisse Leute, die von einem innerlichen Berufe zum Kunstrichteramte genaget werden, meine Arbeit nur deswegen mit dem Englischen zusammen hielten, um Fehler darinnen zu suchen. Diese bitte ich, die harten Gesetze eines deutschen Dichters, wenn er übersetzt, zu bedenken: oder da diese Herren sich von der critischen Billigkeit ziemlich losgesaget haben; so wollen wir uns beyderseits damit trösten, daß es noch bisher *Popens* Schicksal so mit sich gebracht hat, in die Hände schlechter Uebersetzer zu gerathen: welches gar leicht zu erweisen seyn würde.

Einen besondern Zierrath werden dieser Uebersetzung die dabey befindlichen Kupfer geben, welche unsere geschickteste deutsche Künstlerinn, die berühmte *Frau Wernerinn*, erfunden und gezeichnet hat. Sie wird mir es erlauben, daß ich hier öffentlich den Dank abstatte, den ich ihr, für ihre freundschaftsvolle Bemühung schuldig bin; und einen guten Theil des Beyfalls, den dieses Werk hier und da finden möchte, auf die Rechnung ihrer saubern Zeichnungen setze.

Von den beyden Gedichten, die hinten angehängt worden, muß ich noch erinnern, daß ich sie gleichsam aus Rache gegen meinen französischen Uebersetzer, der mir so viel vergebliche Mühe gemacht hat, angehängt habe. Man muß doch den Herren Franzosen einmal zeigen, wie es einem Schriftsteller gefällt, wenn man nach eigner Willkühr mit ihm umgeht. Denn ich gestehe gar gern, daß meine Verse, als eine Uebersetzung, vom Grundtexte gar zu sehr abweichen: als meine eigne Arbeit aber, sehen sie demselben wieder zu ähnlich; so daß ich mich vielleicht mit der *Frau Deshoulieres* lange herum nöthigen würde, wem von uns beyden diese Verse gehören sollten. Doch in den elysischen Feldern können die Poeten gar viel mit einander abmachen; und wir wollen deswegen schon eins werden. Indessen habe ich meine Arbeit wegen dieser mir bewußten Abweichung, eine freye *Uebersetzung* genennet; es ist mir aber leid, daß ich sie nicht eine *französische* genennt habe.

Lebe wohl. Geschrieben an der Leipziger Ostermesse des 1744sten Jahres.

The Rape of the Lock[1]

Canto I.

What dire offence from am'rous causes springs,
What mighty contests rise from trivial things,
I sing — This verse to C–, Muse! is due:
This, ev'n *Belinda* may vouchsafe to view:
Slight is the subject, but not so the praise,
If She inspire, and He approve my lays.
Say what strange motive, Goddess! could compel
A well-bred Lord t' assault a gentle *Belle*?
Oh say what stranger cause, yet unexplor'd,
Cou'd make a gentle *Belle* reject a Lord?
In tasks so bold, can little men engage,
And in soft bosoms dwells such mighty Rage?[2]
Sol thro' white curtains shot a tim'rous ray,[3]
And ope'd those eyes that must eclipse the day;
Now lap-dogs give themselves the rousing shake,
And sleepless lovers, just at twelve, awake:
Thrice rung the bell, the slipper knock'd the ground,
And the press'd watch return'd a silver sound.
Belinda still her downy pillow prest,
Her guardian *Sylph* prolong'd the balmy rest:
'Twas he had summon'd to her silent bed
The morning-dream that hover'd o'er her head.

1. *The first sketch of this Poem was written in less than a fortnight's time, in 1711, in two Canto's, and so printed in a Miscellany, without the name of the Author. The Machines were not inserted till a year after, when he publish'd it, and annex'd the foregoing Dedication.*
2. VER. 11, 12. It was in the first editions,
And dwells such rage in softest bosoms then,
And lodge such daring Souls in little Men?
3. VER. 13, &c. Sol *thro' white curtains did his beams display,*
And ope'd those eyes which brighter shine than they,
Shock *just had giv'n himself the rousing shake,*
And Nymphs prepar'd their Chocolate to take;
Thrice the wrought slipper knock'd against the ground,
And striking watches the tenth hour resound.
First Edit.

Der Lockenraub

Erstes Buch.

Was für strenge Grausamkeiten aus verliebten Quellen gehn;
Was für harte Zänkereyen aus gemeinem Stoff entstehn;
Das besing ich durch dieß Lied. Muse, *Cromweln*[1] sey es eigen:
Möcht auch nur *Belindens*[2] Gunst sich dabey geneigt bezeigen!
Sing ich gleich von schlechtem Stoffe, ist mir doch mein Ruhm beliebt:
Wenn die eine mir Erfindung, und der andre, Beyfall giebt.
Göttinn! welch ein seltner Trieb hat den Zufall doch erreget,
Daß ein wohlgezogner Lord einer Schönen Zorn beweget?
Oder, laß den Grund mich wissen, den kein Mensch entdecken kann:
Warum hat hier eine Schöne einem Lord so weh gethan?
Kann denn eine zarte Brust so viel Grausamkeit besitzen?
Kann so viel Verwegenheit eines Stutzers Herz erhitzen?
Phöbus schoß durch manchen Vorhang einen furchterfüllten Stral,
Und eröffnete die Augen, deren Glanz sein Ansehn stahl.
Mancher Schoßhund regt sich schon, und der Mittagsstunde Schlagen
Schien der Buhler schlaflos Heer aus den Federn aufzujagen.
Dreymal tönete die Glocke[3]; der Pantoffel wird bewegt,
Und durch die gedruckte Sackuhr wird ein Silberton erregt.
Nur *Belinde* lag noch sanft auf die Küssen hingestrecket,
Denn es hatte sie noch nichts aus dem letzten Schlaf erwecket.
Ein ihr zugegebner *Sylphe*[4] hatte dieß mit Fleiß gemacht,
Und den Geist der Morgenträume an ihr stilles Bett gebracht.

1. Diesen Namen habe ich ohne Bedenken hier ausgeschrieben, nachdem ich in *Pope's litterary Correspondence*, die bey Curl 1735 herausgekommen, im 2 Th. a. d. 10. S. einen Brief gefunden, den Herr Pope an diesen Lord, Henrich Cromwell, schreibt; und worinnen er dieser Geschichte Erwähnung thut, auch ihm zu seinem Raube der Locke Glück wünschet.
2. Dieses ist Frau Arabella Fermor gewesen, der das Landhaus gehöret, wo die Gesellschaft, in welcher der ganze Lockenraub begangen worden, sich einige Tage erlustiget hat.
3. Vermuthlich ist es in London, wie an vielen andern Orten gewöhnlich, daß um eilf Uhr eine große Bethglocke dreymal angeschlagen wird.
4. Dieses sind kleine Luftgeister, die ihr erstes Daseyn dem *Comte de Gabalis* zu verdanken haben, nach dessen Vorgeben sie zuweilen die Goldmacher besuchen, um sie wegen der Bücher des *Averroës* um Rath zu fragen, die die Sylphen nicht allemal wohl verstehen. Siehe das Tractätchen *le Comte de Gabalis, ou Entretiens sur les Sciences secrettes, p. m. 13.*

A Youth more glitt'ring than a Birth-night Beau,
(That ev'n in slumber caus'd her cheek to glow)
Seem'd to her ear his winning lips to lay,
And thus in whispers said, or seem'd to say.
Fairest of mortals, thou distinguish'd care
Of thousand bright Inhabitants of Air!
If e'er one Vision touch'd thy infant thought,
Of all the Nurse and all the Priest have taught;
Of airy Elves by moonlight shadows seen,
The silver token, and the circled green,
Or virgins visited by Angel-pow'rs,
With golden crowns and wreaths of heav'nly flow'rs;
Hear and believe! thy own importance know,
Nor bound thy narrow views to things below.
Some secret truths, from learned pride conceal'd,
To Maids alone and Children are reveal'd:
What tho' no credit doubting Wits may give?
The Fair and Innocent shall still believe.
Know then, unnumber'd Spirits round thee fly,
The light Militia of the lower sky;
These, tho' unseen, are ever on the wing,
Hang o'er the Box, and hover round the Ring:
Think what an equipage thou hast in Air,
And view with scorn two Pages and a Chair.
As now your own, our beings were of old,
And once inclos'd in Woman's beauteous mold;
Thence, by a soft transition, we repair
From earthly Vehicles to these of air.
Think not, when Woman's transient breath is fled,
That all her vanities at once are dead:
Succeeding vanities she still regards,
And tho' she plays no more, o'erlooks the cards.
Her joy in gilded Chariots, when alive,[1]
And love of *Ombre*, after death survive.
For when the Fair in all their pride expire,
To their first Elements the Souls retire:
The Sprites of fiery Termagants in Flame
Mount up, and take a *Salamander's* name.
Soft yielding minds to Water glide away,

1. VER. 54, 55. — *Quæ gratia currum*
Armorumque fuit vivis, quæ cura nitentes
Pascere equos, eadem sequitur tellure repostos.
Virg. Æn. 6.

Ihr erscheint ein junger Herr, schöner als ein Stutzer siehet,
Daß *Belinden* auch im Schlaf eine Schamröth überziehet.
Dessen schmeichelhafte Lippen, denen man nichts weigern kann,
Schienen ihr ins Ohr zu lispeln, oder huben wirklich an:
„Allerschönste dieser Erden! auserlesner Gegenstand
„Heitrer Geister, deren Anzahl in der Luft die Wohnung fand.
„Hat dir jemals, als ein Kind, manche Phantasie behaget,
„Die der Priesterorden lehrt, und die Ammen dir gesaget,
„Von den leichten Poltergeistern, die man nur bey Mondschein sieht;
„Von dem wutherfüllten Heere, welches durch die Wälder zieht;
„Von den Dirnen, die Besuch von den Engeln selbst, empfangen,
„Die mit Kronen ganz von Gold, und mit Himmelsblumen, prangen:
„O so hör, und gieb mir Beyfall! Lerne deinen eignen Werth:
„Klebe nicht an niedern Dingen, deren Last den Geist beschwert.
„Was gelehrter Stolz nicht faßt, was die Weisen nicht verstehen,
„Können junge Kinder nur, und das Frauenzimmer sehen:
„Was der Grübler Witz nicht glaubet, was für sie ein Räthsel war,
„Bleibt allein der zarten Unschuld und der Schönheit sonnenklar.
„Lerne denn: ein Geisterheer hält beständig dich umgeben,
„Dessen Körper in der Luft als ein leichtes Kriegsvolk schweben.
„Dieß ist ungesehn zugegen, folget dir auf jedem Schritt,
„Flattert über dir im Schauplatz, eilt auch in Gesellschaft mit.
„Denk an dieß Gefolge stets, das du in der Luft kannst haben,
„Und verachte Kutsch und Pferd mit zween blanken Edelknaben.
„Was du bist, sind wir gewesen. In der englischen Gestalt
„Angenehmer Frauenbilder war sonst unser Aufenthalt;
„Als wir aber nach der Zeit dieser irdnen Hütt' entgangen,
„Haben wir in freyer Luft einen reinern Leib empfangen.
„Glaube nicht, wenn eine Schöne hier auf eurem Erdball stirbt,
„Daß ihr ganzes eitles Wesen durch den letzten Hauch verdirbt.
„Nein; der Wechsel alter Lust kann ihr Auge noch verblenden,
„Und das Spiel ergetzt sie noch, ist es gleich in fremden Händen.
„Ihre Lust zur Lomberkarte, und zu goldner Kutschen Pracht,
„Hat das Sterben selber ihnen noch nicht aus dem Kopf gebracht:
„Denn, sobald sich nur ihr Geist voller Stolz vom Leibe trennte,
„Zog er sich sogleich zurück, zu dem ersten Elemente.
„Sterben nämlich wilde Weiber; so entweicht ihr Poltergeist
„Mit den Flammen in die Höhe, wo er *Salamander*[1] heißt.
„Ein gefälliges Gemüth sehn wir in die Fluthen sinken;

1. Dieses sind nach dem *Comte de Gabalis* die Einwohner der Feuerregion, die zwischen dem Kreise des Monden, und zwischen unserer Luft seyn soll. Sie dienen den Goldmachern; allein sie sehnen sich nicht sehr nach ihrer Gesellschaft. Siehe den *Comte de Gabalis p. m. 25*.

And sip, with *Nymphs*, their elemental Tea.
The graver Prude sinks downward to a *Gnome*,
In search of mischief still on Earth to roam.
The light Coquettes in *Sylphs* aloft repair,
And sport and flutter in the fields of Air.
Know farther yet; whoever fair and chaste
Rejects mankind, is by some *Sylph* embrac'd:
For Spirits, freed from mortal laws, with ease
Assume what sexes and what shapes they please.
What guards the purity of melting Maids
In courtly balls, and midnight masquerades,
Safe from the treach'rous friend, the daring spark,
The glance by day, the whisper in the dark,
When kind occasion prompts their warm desires,
When music softens, and when dancing fires?
'Tis but their *Sylph*, the wise Celestials know,
Tho' *Honour* is the word with Men below.
Some nymphs there are, too conscious of their face,
For life predestin'd to the *Gnomes* embrace.
These swell their prospects and exalt their pride,
When offers are disdain'd, and love deny'd:
Then gay Ideas croud the vacant brain,
While Peers and Dukes, and all their sweeping train,
And Garters, Stars, and Coronets appear,
And in soft sounds, *Your Grace* salutes their ear.
'Tis these that early taint the female soul,
Instruct the eyes of young Coquettes to roll,
Teach Infants cheeks a bidden blush to know,
And little hearts to flutter at a Beau.
Oft' when the world imagine women stray,
The *Sylphs* thro' mystic mazes guide their way,
Thro' all the giddy circle they pursue,
And old impertinence expel by new.

„Um in diesem Element mit den *Nymphen*[1] Thee zu trinken.
„Spröde stürzen zu den *Gnomen*[2], in der Erden finstre Kluft,
„Suchen Bosheit auszuüben, und durchkreuzen manche Gruft.
„Ein verbuhltes eitles Weib wird den *Sylphen* zugestellet,
„Schwärmt in freyer Luft herum, scherzt und spielt, wies ihm gefället.
„Lerne ferner: Eine Schöne, die aus Keuschheit Männer haßt,
„Wird von irgend einem *Sylphen* in verschwiegner Luft umfaßt.
„Denn, von Menschenkörpern frey, ändern wir auch unsre Leiber,
„Werden, wie es uns beliebt, heute Männer, morgen Weiber.
„Was beschützt die zarten Herzen, denen man viel Netze stellt,
„Wenn man irgend Bälle giebet, nächtlich Mummereyen hält?
„Was bedeckt sie vor Verrath, vor verwegner Buhler Blicken,
„Die bey Nacht geschwätzig sind, und des Tages schlau bestricken;
„Wenn Gelegenheit und Lockung sie zu Leidenschaften führt,
„Die Musik sie weichlich machet, und der frohe Tanz sie rührt?
„Bloß ihr *Sylphe* wirket dieß! dieses wissen unsre Chöre;
„Aber bey euch Sterblichen nennt man es den Trieb der Ehre.
„Solche *Nymphen*, die aus Hochmuth ihr Gesicht zu hoch geschätzt,
„Sind schon lebend bösen *Gnomen* zur Umarmung ausgesetzt.
„Diese Geister wissen früh ihren Hochmuth zu erhöhen,
„Daß kein Liebesantrag gilt, und kein Freyer kann bestehen.
„Dann erfüllen bunte Bilder ihren leeren Kopf mit Wind,
„Wenn sich *Pair* und *Herzog* zeigen, die am Staate prächtig sind;
„Wenn, bey Stern und Ordensband *Excellenzen* selbst es wagen,
„Mit gelindem sanftem Ton ihnen was ins Ohr zu sagen.
„Ihre Kunst ists, die so zeitig junge Mädchen klüglich lehrt,
„Wie bey schlauen Buhlerinnen sich das Auge recht verkehrt;
„Wie ein falsches Schamroth schon Kinderwangen überziehet;
„Wie das Herze klopfen muß, wenn es einen Stutzer siehet.
„Oftmals pflegt die Welt zu glauben, eine Schöne sey verirrt,
„Da sie doch ihr *Sylphe* leitet, daß kein Abweg sie verwirrt;
„Der sie durch der Buhler Heer, als durch schnelle Wirbel, rücket,
„Und durch neue Thorheit, oft einer alten Wuchs, ersticket.

1. Diese Nymphen sind die Einwohner der Flüsse und Meere. Die alten Weisen oder Goldmacher haben sie *Ondiens* oder Nymphen genennt. Es giebt wenig männliche unter ihnen; die Weiber aber sind ungemein viel schöner, als die Töchter der Menschen. *Le Comte de Gabalis, p. m. 24. 25.*
2. Diese Gnomen sind die Einwohner der Erden, fast bis zu ihrem Mittelpuncte. Sie bewachen die Schätze, die Bergwerke und Edelgesteine. Sie schaffen den Schülern der Goldmacher so viel Geld, als sie brauchen, und gehen seltsam gekleidet. *Le Comte de Gabalis, p. m. 25.*

What tender maid but must a victim fall
To one man's treat, but for another's ball?
When *Florio* speaks, what virgin could withstand,
If gentle *Damon* did not squeeze her hand?
With varying vanities, from ev'ry part,
They shift the moving Toyshop of their heart;
Where wigs with wigs, with sword-knots sword-knots strive,
Beaus banish beaus, and coaches coaches drive.
This erring mortals Levity may call,
Oh blind to truth! the *Sylphs* contrive it all.
Of these am I, who thy protection claim,
A watchful sprite, and *Ariel* is my name.
Late, as I rang'd the crystal wilds of air,
In the clear Mirror of thy ruling Star
I saw, alas! some dread event impend,
E'er to the main this morning sun descend.
But heav'n reveals not what, or how, or where:
Warn'd by the *Sylph*, oh pious maid, beware!
This to disclose is all thy guardian can.
Beware of all, but most beware of Man!
He said; when *Shock*, who thought she slept too long,
Leap'd up, and wak'd his mistress with his tongue.
'Twas then *Belinda*, if report say true,
Thy eyes first open'd on a Billet-doux;
Wounds, Charms, and Ardors, were no sooner read,
But all the Vision vanish'd from thy head.
And now, unveil'd, the Toilet stands display'd,
Each silver Vase in mystic order laid.
First, robe'd in white, the nymph intent adores
With head uncover'd, the Cosmetic pow'rs.
A heav'nly Image in the glass appears,
To that she bends, to that her eyes she rears;
Th' inferior Priestess, at her altar's side,
Trembling, begins the sacred rites of Pride.
Unnumber'd treasures ope at once, and here
The various off'rings of the world appear;
From each she nicely culls with curious toil,
And decks the Goddess with the glitt'ring spoil.
This casket *India's* glowing gems unlocks,
And all *Arabia* breathes from yonder box.
The Tortoise here and Elephant unite,
Transform'd to combs, the speckled, and the white.

„Welches zarte Mädchen würde durch ein Gastmahl nicht gefällt;
„Hätt ein andrer, ihr zu Ehren, Tanz und Lust nicht angestellt?
„Wenn der schöne *Damon* spricht, welches Herz würd nicht bestricket;
„Stünde *Thirsis* nicht dabey, der ihr sanft die Hände drücket?
„Mit so vielen Eitelkeiten treiben sie ein muntres Herz,
„Kreiseln gleich, nach allen Seiten, drehn es vor und hinterwärts:
„Wenn Perrücken streitig sind, wo die Degenbänder kämpfen,
„Stutzer wider Stutzer stehn, oder Kutschen, Kutschen dämpfen.
„Blöder Menschen Dünkel glaubet, daß dieß lauter Leichtsinn ist:
„Wie verfehlt man hier der Wahrheit! alles wirkt der *Sylphen* List.
„Ich bin auch von dieser Zahl, und mein Wachen schützt dein Leben,
„Die Benennung, *Ariel*, hat das Schicksal mir gegeben.
„Als ich die crystallnen Felder reiner Lüfte jüngst durchspürt,
„Sah ich in den hellen Spiegel des Gestirns, das dich regiert.
„Hier erblickt ich nun ein Weh! über deiner Scheitel hangen,
„Dessen Drohung zu vollziehn, Phöbus heut hervorgegangen.
„Aber wie? und wo? und welches? das verbirgt des Schicksals Macht.
„Sey gewarnt von deinem *Sylphen*! frommes Kind, nimm dich in acht!
„Alles was dein Schutzgeist kann, ist, dir dieses zu entdecken:
„Heute muß dich alles zwar, sonderlich das Mannsvolk, schrecken!
Also sprach er; doch dem Hündchen dünkt *Belindens* Schlaf zu lang,
So, daß seine Schmeichelzunge plötzlich ihren Traum verdrang.
Schöne! wo der Ruff nicht triegt, mußten die verliebten Zeilen
Von *Silvanders* Hand, zuerst, deines Schlummers Rest vertheilen.
Wunden, Schmerzen, Pein und Sehnsucht hast du kaum darinn erblickt,
O so ist in deinem Kopfe Traum und Warnung ganz erstickt.
Jetzt bemerkt man, daß ihr Fuß zum enthüllten Nachttisch gehet,
Wo manch silbernes Gefäß in verborgner Ordnung stehet.
Sie verehrt, mit bloßem Haupte, und in einer weißen Tracht,
Das kosmetische Vermögen, das die Schönheit reizend macht.
Sie erblickt ein himmlisch Bild, das auf hellem Glase schwebet,
Und zu dem sich ehrfurchtsvoll ihrer Augen Stral erhebet.
Eine mindre Opferschwester macht sich, mit gebognem Knie,
Zitternd zu des Altars Seiten, an des Putzwerks Liturgie.
Hundert Schachteln öffnen sich, mit den ungezählten Schätzen
Aller Opfer der Natur, die der Menschen Stolz ergetzen.
Fast aus jeder wird mit Sorgfalt etwas glänzendes geklaubt;
Und der Raub des ganzen Erdballs decket nun der Göttinn Haupt.
Indiens geschliffnen Kies sieht man häufig hier erscheinen,
Ganz *Arabien* dampft auch, mitten unter Edelsteinen.
Das Gehäuse großer Kröten, und der Elephantenzahn,
Haben sich allhier als Kämme, bunt und weiß, hervorgethan.

Here files of pins extend their shining rows,
Puffs, Powder, Patches, Bibles, Billet-doux.
Now awful Beauty puts on all its arms;
The fair each moment rises in her charms,
Repairs her smiles, awakens ev'ry grace,
And calls forth all the wonders of her face;
Sees by degrees a purer blush arise,
And keener lightnings quicken in her eyes.
The busy *Sylphs* surround their darling care,[1]
These set the head, and those divide the hair,
Some fold the sleeve, whilst others plait the gown;
And *Betty's* prais'd for labours not her own.

Canto II.

Not with more glories, in th' etherial plain,
The Sun first rises o'er the purpled main,
Than issuing forth, the rival of his beams
Lanch'd on the bosom of the silver *Thames*.
Fair Nymphs, and well-drest Youths around her shone,
But ev'ry eye was fix'd on her alone.
On her white breast a sparkling Cross she wore,
Which Jews might kiss, and Infidels adore.
Her lively looks a sprightly mind disclose,
Quick as her eyes, and as unfix'd as those:
Favours to none, to all she smiles extends,
Oft' she rejects, but never once offends.
Bright as the sun, her eyes the gazers strike,
And, like the sun, they shine on all alike.
Yet graceful ease, and sweetness void of pride
Might hide her faults, if *Belles* had faults to hide:
If to her share some female errors fall,
Look on her face, and you'll forget 'em all.

1. VER. 145. *The busy* Sylphs, & c.] Antient Traditions of the *Rabbi's* relate, that several of the fallen Angels became amorous of Women, and particularize some; among the rest *Asael*, who lay with *Naamah*, the wife of *Noah*, or of *Ham*; and who continuing impenitent, still presides over the Women's Toilets. *Bereshi Rabbi* in *Genes*. 6. 2.

Dichtgesteckter Nadeln Heer straft in reinen Silberflammen;
Puder, Schönfleck, Liebesbrief, Bibel, alles liegt beysammen!
Als nunmehr die seltne Schöne zu den stärksten Waffen greift,
Sieht man, wie sich nach einander Reizung über Reizung häuft;
Wie das Lächeln lebhaft wird, nebst der Anmuth ihrer Minen;
Bis die ganze Wunderkraft ihres Angesichts erschienen.
Endlich muß auf ihren Wangen ein geläutert Roth entstehn,
Und aus ihren heitern Blicken müssen schärfre Stralen gehn.
Manches *Sylphen* treuer Fleiß will an seiner Müh nichts sparen:
Dieser setzt den Kopfputz auf; jener künstelt an den Haaren;
Einer faltet ihr den Aermel, wie die andern Rock und Kleid:
Sylvia bekömmt den Lobspruch für der *Sylphen* Aemsigkeit.

Ende des ersten Buches.

Das zweyte Buch.

Phöbus hat nicht halb die Pracht, wenn er sich am Himmel zeiget,
Da er nach verstrichner Nacht aus dem Purpurmeere steiget,
Als die reizende *Belinde* ihm zum Trotze hier erwies,
Da sie auf der *Themse* Silber von dem glatten Ufer stieß.
Schöne *Nymphen* sah man hier, goldne *Stutzer* um sie stehen;
Doch ein jeder sah nur sie, weiter mochte man nichts sehen.
Auf dem weißgewölbten Busen hieng ein Kreuz von großem Werth:
Rabbi Mauschel hätts geküßet, und ein Heid als Gott verehrt.
Ihrer Blicke Munterkeit zeigt ein feuerreich Gemüthe,
Schnell, wie ihrer Augen Paar, und gleich wandelbar an Güte.
Jeden weis sie anzulächeln, keiner kriegt die Gunst allein;
Oft versagt sie, doch auch dadurch wird kein Mensch beleidigt seyn.
Gleich der Sonnen, pflegt ihr Blick jeden, der sie sieht, zu laben;
Gleich der Sonnen, läßt sie auch alle gleichen Vortheil haben.
Huld und Anmuth sonder Hochmuth deckt bey ihr der Fehler Heer;
Wenn ein Fehler bey den Schönen zu bedecken nöthig wär.
Oder wird noch ein Versehn des Geschlechts ihr beygemessen[1]:
O so schaut ihr Antlitz nur; alsobald ist es vergessen.

1. Ich kann nicht umhin, hier ein Beyspiel von der Nachläßigkeit des französischen Uebersetzers zu geben, um dasjenige zu rechtfertigen, was ich in der Vorrede gesaget habe. Er hat diese Stelle ganz verkehrt übersetzt, indem er sagt: 'Ces petits defauts même sont sur le compte de son sexe'. *Ihre kleinen Fehler selbst werden auf die Rechnung ihres Geschlechts gesetzt.* Herr Pope sagt gerade das Widerspiel. Er gesteht noch nicht einmal zu, daß sie Fehler habe; sondern er sagt nur, *wenn man ihr irgend ein Versehn des Geschlechts beymessen oder zuschreiben sollte,*

If to her share some female errors fall.

Uebrigens bemerke ich hier im Vorbeygehen, daß die Armuth der französischen Sprache

This Nymph, to the destruction of mankind,
Nourish'd two Locks, which graceful hung behind
In equal curls, and well conspir'd to deck
With shining ringlets the smooth iv'ry neck:
Love in these labyrinths his slaves detains,
And mighty hearts are held in slender chains.
With hairy sprindges we the birds betray,
Slight lines of hair surprize the finny prey,
Fair tresses man's imperial race insnare,
And beauty draws us with a single hair.
Th' advent'rous Baron the bright locks admir'd,
He saw, he wish'd, and to the prize aspir'd.
Resolv'd to win, he meditates the way,
By force to ravish, or by fraud betray;
For when success a Lover's toil attends,
Few ask, if fraud or force attain'd his ends.
For this, e'er *Phœbus* rose, he had implor'd
Propitious heav'n, and ev'ry pow'r ador'd,
But chiefly Love — to Love an altar built,
Of twelve vast *French* Romances, neatly gilt.
There lay three garters, half a pair of gloves;
And all the trophies of his former loves.
With tender Billet-doux he lights the pyre,
And breathes three am'rous sighs to raise the fire.
Then prostrate falls, and begs with ardent eyes
Soon to obtain, and long possess the prize:
The pow'rs gave ear, and granted half his pray'r,[1]
The rest, the winds dispers'd in empty air.
But now secure the painted vessel glides,
The sun-beams trembling on the floating tydes;
While melting music steals upon the sky,
And soften'd sounds along the waters die;
Smooth flow the waves, the Zephyrs gently play,
Belinda smil'd, and all the world was gay.
All but the *Sylph* — with careful thoughts opprest,

1. Virg. Æn. II.

Zum Verderben aller Männer, hieng von ihres Hauptes Haar
Ein Paar Locken, das nach hinten zierlich aufgerollet war,
Und in gleicher Krümme lag, um, mit stralenreichen Ringeln
Einen Hals von Elfenbein desto schöner zu umzingeln.
Dieses sind die Labyrinthe, wo die Liebe Sklaven fällt,
Und mit solchen dünnen Ketten auch die stärksten Herzen hält.
Oftmals pflegt ein hären Netz das Geflügel zu bestricken,
Und ein dünnes Garn von Haar leichtes Flußvolk zu berücken.
Auch der Mensch, der Herr des Erdballs, kömmt durch Locken in Gefahr;
Ja der Schönheit Macht verführt uns oftmals durch ein einzig Haar.

Der verwegene *Baron*, den der Locken Reiz gefangen,
Sieht sie, wünscht sie, und wird kühn, dieses Kleinod zu erlangen.
Er entschließt sich zum Gewinnen, und besinnt sich voller Müh,
Wie er sie mit Macht erhalte, oder mit Betrug entzieh.
Denn ein Buhler, den ein Lohn zu beliebter Arbeit zwinget,
Fragt nicht, ists Gewalt, ists List? wenn sein Endzweck nur gelinget.

Darum rief er, eh sich *Phöbus* morgens noch hervorgethan,
Jede gunsterfüllte Gottheit, und den Himmel, brünstig an.
Doch der Lieb insonderheit sieht man den Altar errichten,
Aus zwölf dicken, gallischen, nettverguldten Liebsgeschichten.
Anderthalb Paar Hosenbänder, und ein halb Paar Handschuh schier,
Alle seine Siegeszeichen alter Liebe, liegen hier.
Statt des Holzes trägt er schnell manchen Liebesbrief zusammen,
Drey verliebter Seufzer Hauch bringt sie alsobald in Flammen.
Hierauf fällt er kniend nieder, und erbittet sehnsuchtsvoll:
Daß der Preis ihm bald gelingen, und ihn lang erfreuen soll!
Amor hörts: doch wird sein Flehn ihm zur Hälfte nur gewähret;
Weil der andre Theil verfliegt, und in freyer Luft zerfähret.

Nun schwamm das gemalte Fahrzeug sicher auf der Silberfluth,
Und auf der bewegten Fläche spielt mit Zittern Phöbus Glut:
Da der Tonkunst sanftes Spiel aller Hörer Lob erwirbet,
Und der süßen Seyten Hall auf dem heitern Wasser stirbet.

Still und sanft spielt Well und Welle; jeder *Zephir* spielt auch so:
Denn man sieht *Belinden* lachen, und die ganze Welt wird froh.
Alle Welt; nur nicht ihr *Sylph*. Jener Ausspruch macht ihm Sorgen;

in Beywörtern, auch dieses geistreiche Gedicht, in der ersten Uebersetzung, sehr matt gemacht hat. Ich könnte bey diesem Absatze fast bey jeder Zeile ein Exempel davon geben. Ich will aber nur gleich die zwey ersten Zeilen nehmen:

Not with more glories, in th'eternal plain
The sun first rises o'er the purpled main;

die der französische Uebersetzer bloß durch 'le soleil sortant de l'onde', *die Sonne, die aus dem Meere hervorstieg*, gegeben. Das klingt nun wahrlich sehr matt für den feurigen Pope.

Th' impending woe sate heavy on his breast.
He summons strait his Denizens of air;
The lucid squadrons round the sails repair:
Soft o'er the shrouds aerial whispers breathe,
That seem'd but Zephyrs to the train beneath.
Some to the sun their insect-wings unfold,
Waft on the breeze, or sink in clouds of gold;
Transparent forms, too fine for mortal sight,
Their fluid bodies half dissolv'd in light.
Loose to the wind their airy garments flew,
Thin glitt'ring textures of the filmy dew,
Dipt in the richest tincture of the skies,
Where light disports in ever-mingling dyes,
While ev'ry beam new transient colours flings,
Colours that change whene'er they wave their wings.
Amid the circle, on the gilded mast,
Superior by the head, was *Ariel* plac'd;
His purple pinions opening to the sun,
He rais'd his azure wand, and thus begun.
Ye *Sylphs* and *Sylphids*, to your chief give ear,
Fays, *Fairies*, *Genii*, *Elves*, and *Dæmons* hear!
Ye know the spheres and various talks assign'd
By laws eternal to th' aerial kind.
Some in the fields of purest *Æther* play,
And bask and whiten in the blaze of day.
Some guide the course of wand'ring orbs on high,
Or roll the planets thro' the boundless sky.
Some less refin'd, beneath the moon's pale light
Pursue the stars that shoot athwart the night,
Or suck the mists in grosser air below,
Or dip their pinions in the painted bow,
Or brew fierce tempests on the wintry main,
Or o'er the glebe distill the kindly rain.
Others on earth o'er the human race preside,

Darum liegt in seiner Brust ein geheimer Schmerz verborgen.
Alles Volk der höhern Kreise lockt er aus der obern Luft;
Und dieß leuchtende Geschwader kömmt, so bald der Sylphe ruft.
An dem Tauwerk merket man das Gelispel dieser Chöre;
Doch im Boote glaubet man, daß man nur den *Zephyr* höre.
Alles schlägt die dünnen Flügel durch den hellen Sonnenschein,
Senkt sich in die kühlen Lüfte oder goldnen Wolken ein.
Dieser Geister lustger Leib ist zu fein für unser Sehen,
Ein so flüßig Körperchen kann vom Lichtstral schon zergehen.
Ihr ganz offnes klares Kleidchen ist von zartes Thaues Haut,
Das man mit den dünnen Lüften nach Belieben flattern schaut.
In der schönsten Wolken Naß wirds zum Färben eingetauchet,
Daß ein immerscheinend Licht in die zarten Fasern hauchet.
Da ein jeder Stral indessen neuer Farben Glanz durchweht,
Die sich nach der Art verändern, wie der Geist die Flügel dreht.
Auf dem reichvergoldten Mast ließ sich mitten unter allen,
Kopfes länger als die Schaar, *Ariel* den Sitz gefallen:
Und als er die Purpurschwingen zu der Sonnen aufgethan,
Schwang er den saphirnen Zepter, und fieng so zu reden an:
„Hört, was euer Haupt befiehlt, o ihr *Sylphen* und *Sylphiden*,
„*Hexen*, *Zaubrer*, *Poltergeist*, *Alp*, und was ich herbeschieden.
„Was ein ewiges Gesetze uns für Pflichten zugewandt,
„Die wir in den Lüften wohnen, ist euch allen ganz bekannt.
„Manchen sieht man voller Lust in den reinsten Lüften schwärmen;
„Um sich an des Tages Glut, theils zu bleichen, theils zu wärmen.
„Mancher führt die Wanderkugeln in der ungemeßnen Höh;
„Oder rollet den Planeten, daß er in dem Gleise geh.
„Mancher Dümmre hascht des Nachts, bey des Mondes falbem Schimmer,
„Jeden Stern im Fallen auf; flattert stets, und fängt ihn nimmer.
„Aus der gröbern Luft von unten sauget[1] der den Nebel ein,
„Oder tunket seine Schwingen in des Regenbogens Schein.
„Oder braut ein Ungestüm, um die Wintersee zu rühren;
„Oder muß für Erd und Land sanfte Regen distilliren.
„Andrer Herrschaft sorgt auf Erden für das menschliche Geschlecht,

1. Diese zwo Zeilen hat der französische Uebersetzer ganz verkehrt gegeben. Er übersetzt des Pope Worte:

Or suck the Mists in grosser Air below
Or dip their Pinions in the painted Bow;

so: 'de former les brouïllards de l'air le plus grossier; que d'autres peignent l'Iris'; *sie bereiten aus der dicksten Luft den Nebel, und andere malen den Regenbogen.* Doch was sage ich? Pope läßt die Luftgeister ein Ungestüm in der Wintersee brauen, sein Uebersetzer läßt es kneten, 'ils petrissent les tempêtes'.

Watch all their ways, and all their actions guide:
Of these the chief the care of Nations own,
And guard with Arms divine the *British* Throne.
Our humbler province is to tend the Fair;
Not a less pleasing, tho' less glorious care:
To save the powder from too rude a gale,
Nor let th' imprison'd essences exhale;
To draw fresh colours from the vernal flow'rs;
To steal from rainbows e'er they drop in show'rs
A brighter wash; to curl their waving hairs,
Assist their blushes, and inspire their airs;
Nay oft', in dreams, invention we bestow,
To change a Flounce, or add a Furbelow.
This day, black Omens threat the brightest Fair
That e'er deserv'd a watchful spirit's care;
Some dire disaster, or by force, or slight;
But what, or where, the fates have wrapt in night.
Whether the nymph shall break *Diana's* law,
Or some frail *China* jar receive a flaw,
Or stain her honour, or her new brocade,
Forget her pray'rs, or miss a masquerade,
Or lose her heart, or necklace, at a ball;
Or whether Heav'n has doom'd that *Shock* must fall.
Haste then, ye spirits! to your charge repair;
The flutt'ring fan be *Zephyretta's* care;
The drops to thee, *Brillante*, we consign;
And, *Momentilla*, let the watch be thine;
Do thou, *Crispissa*, tend her fav'rite Lock:
Ariel himself shall be the guard of *Shock*.
To fifty chosen *Sylphs*, of special note,
We trust th' important charge, the Petticoat:
Oft' have we known that seven-fold fence to fail,

„Wacht für dessen Thun und Lassen, lenket seine Thaten recht.
„Die erhabensten hiervon[1] müssen ganzen Völkern nützen,
„Und mit göttergleichem Arm auch der Britten Thron beschützen.
„Unser aller leichtre Pflichten sind der Schönen Sicherheit;
„Diese sind zwar nicht so rühmlich, doch von größrer Lieblichkeit:
„Daß kein gar zu rauher Wind in den leichten Puder hauche;
„Daß der eingesperrte Duft der Essenzen nicht verrauche;
„Daß wir frische Farben holen, von der Frühlingsblumen Pracht;
„An des Regenbogens Nässe, eh er große Tropfen macht,
„Einen Diebstahl zu begehn; ihre Locken aufzurollen;
„Ihrer Schamröth beyzustehn, wenn sie ehrbar scheinen wollen;
„Ja, daß jede Nacht im Träumen eine neue Mode heckt,
„Wie man hier ein Fältchen leget, dort ein neues Schleifchen steckt.
„Aber ach! der Schönsten soll heut ein Unfall widerfahren,
„Die vor allen würdig ist, daß die *Sylphen* sie bewahren.
„Ein nur gar zu harter Unstern droht ihr Arglist oder Macht:
„Aber was, und wo es seyn wird? das verbirgt des Schicksals Nacht.
„Ob die *Nymphe* irgend eins von *Dianens* Grundgesetzen,
„Oder nur ein dünn Gefäß der *Chineser*, wird verletzen?
„Wird vielleicht ihr Ruhm beflecket, oder ihr neu goldnes Kleid?
„Oder das Gebeth vergessen, oder eine Lustbarkeit?
„Wird sie auf dem Ball ihr Herz, oder Halsband[2] nur vermissen?
„Oder wird durch höhern Schluß ihr der Hund vom Schooß geschmissen?
„Auf demnach, ihr Geister alle! wacht und sorgt bey der Gefahr!
„*Zephirette*, nimm der Flächen des bewegten Fächers wahr.
„Du, *Brillante*, sollst den Schmuck in den Ohren treu bewachen.
„*Momentilla* soll sich nicht von der goldnen Sackuhr machen.
„Du, *Crispissa*, stell dich plötzlich bey den liebsten Locken ein;
„Und ich *Ariel* will selber ihres Hündchens Wächter seyn.
„Funfzig *Sylphen* beßrer Art, auf die wir das meiste bauen,
„Wollen wir die schwere Hut ihres Unterrocks vertrauen.
„Dieses siebenfache Bollwerk widersteht nicht stets der List,

1. Aus diesen zwo Zeilen hat der Uebersetzer ein rechtes Mischmasch gemacht. Er sagt: 'Pendant que les Chefs, avec des armées puissantes gouvernent les Nations, soutiennent les Monarchies, et fondent les Empires'. *Indem die Vornehmsten von ihnen mit mächtigen Kriegsheeren*: das sagt Pope nicht; er sagt 'with arms divine', *mit göttlichen Armen*. (Ich weis auch nicht, wo die Sylphen die großen Kriegsheere hernehmen wollten.) *die Völker beherrschen, die Monarchien unterstützen*. (Das sagt Pope nicht; er sagt nur,) 'the Brittish Throne', *und Kaiserthümer stiften*. Davon sagt Pope kein Wort.
2. Auf diesem *Halsbande* hat der Uebersetzer für gut befunden, einen *Fächer* zu machen, und die folgende Zeile hat er gar weggelassen. Vielleicht aus eben der unzeitigen Scheu, warum er in dem ersten Buche die Zeile weggelassen:
   Was der Priesterorden lehrt, und die Ammen dir gesaget.

Tho' stiff with hoops, and arm'd with ribs of whale.
Form a strong line about the silver bound,
And guard the wide circumference around.
Whatever spirit, careless of his charge,
His post neglects, or leaves the fair at large,
Shall feel sharp vengeance soon o'ertake his sins,
Be stop'd in vials, or transfix'd with pins;
Or plung'd in lakes of bitter washes lie,
Or wedg'd whole ages in a bodkin's eye:
Gums and Pomatums shall his flight restrain,
While clog'd he beats his silken wings in vain;
Or Alom stypticks with contracting pow'r
Shrink his thin essence like a rivell'd flow'r:
Or as *Ixion* fix'd, the wretch shall feel
The giddy motion of the whirling Mill,
In fumes of burning Chocolate shall glow,
And tremble at the sea that froaths below!
He spoke; the spirits from the sails descend;
Some, orb in orb, around the nymph extend;
Some thrid the mazy ringlets of her hair;
Some hang upon the pendants of her ear;
With beating hearts the dire event they wait,
Anxious, and trembling for the birth of Fate.

Canto III.

Close by those meads, for ever crown'd with flow'rs,
Where *Thames* with pride surveys his rising tow'rs,
There stands a structure of majestic frame,
Which from the neighb'ring *Hampton* takes its name.
Here *Britain's* statesmen oft the fall foredoom
Of foreign Tyrants, and of Nymphs at home;
Here thou, great ANNA! whom three realms obey,
Dost sometimes counsel take — and sometimes Tea.

„Ob es gleich durch Wallfischribben und durch Reifen furchtbar ist.
„Um den breiten Silbersaum stellet euch in dichtem Kreise,
„Und bewacht dieß weite Rund nach gewissenhafter Weise.
„Welcher *Sylphe* nun aus Leichtsinn seine Pflicht zu schläfrig treibt,
„Von dem strengen Posten weichet, oder nicht stets bey ihr bleibt,
„Der soll sein Verbrechen bald mit der schärfsten Strafe büßen:
„Den sperrt man in Flaschen ein; Nadeln sollen ihn durchspießen;
„Er soll in den tiefen Boden einer trüben Pfütze gehn;
„Oder in den Nadelöhren manch Jahrhundert Schildwacht stehn.
„Seiner leichten Schwingen Kraft soll Pomad und Harz verkleben;
„Und der seidnen Flügel Paar sich zum Flug umsonst bestreben.
„Mit verstopfenden Alaunen wird man ihn zusammen ziehn,
„Bis sein welker Leib verschrumpfet und wie Blumen wird verblühn.
„Oder solch ein Frevler soll, beym Geknirsch der Caffeemühlen,
„Einen schwindelvollen Schwung, so wie dort *Ixion* fühlen.
„In dem Dampf der Chocolade soll er fast vor Brand vergehn,
„Und dieß Meer zu seinen Füßen, voller Zittern, prudeln sehn.
Dieses sagt er: und die Schaar eilet zu des Fahrzeugs Grunde.
Stellet sich in dichten Kreis um Belinden in die Runde.
Dieser macht sich zu den Locken, die ihr schöner Hals besitzt;
Jener hängt sich an das Putzwerk, das in ihren Ohren blitzt.
Jedem pocht das bange Herz vor dem nahen Ungelücke,
Voller Angst erwarten sie die Erfüllung vom Geschicke.

Ende des zweyten Buches.

Das dritte Buch.

Mitten in der schönen Flur, die ein steter Frühling schmücket,
Wo die *Themse* voller Stolz ihrer Thürme Höh erblicket,
Steht ein herrliches Gebäude majestätisch ausgeziert,
Das vom nahgelegnen *Hampton* den berühmten Namen führt.
Mancher Staatsmann sieht allhier, mit besonders schlauen Sinnen,
Auswärts der Tyrannen Fall, und der Nymphen Fall[1] von innen.
Hier, Regentinn dreyer Reiche, *Anna*, groß zu Land und See,
Pflegst du oftmals Rath zu hören, und zuweilen trinkst du Thee.

1. So leichtfertig diese Stelle im Originale klingt, so matt, oder gar falsch hat der französische Uebersetzer dieselbe gegeben. Er sagt: ‘c’est la que les Ministres Britanniques reglent le destin des Etats de l’Europe’. *Hier richten die brittischen Staatsmänner das Schicksal von Europa ein.* Heißt das aber:

Here Britains Statesmen oft the fall foredoom
Of foreign Tyrants, and of Nymphs at home?

Hither the heroes and the nymphs resort,
To taste a while the pleasures of a Court;
In various talk th' instructive hours they past,
Who gave the ball, or paid the visit last;[1]
One speaks the glory of the *British* Queen,
And one describes a charming *Indian* screen;
A third interprets motions, looks, and eyes;
At ev'ry word a reputation dies.
Snuff, or the fan, supply each pause of chat,
With singing, laughing, ogling, and all that.
Mean while declining from the noon of day,
The sun obliquely shoots his burning ray;
The hungry Judges soon the sentence sign,
And wretches hang that jury-men may dine;
The merchant from th' *Exchange* returns in peace,
And the long labours of the Toilet cease.
Belinda now, whom thirst of fame invites,
Burns to encounter two advent'rous Knights,
At *Ombre* singly to decide their doom;
And swells her breast with conquests yet to come.
Strait the three bands prepare in arms to join,
Each band the number of the sacred nine.
Soon as she spreads her hand, th' aerial guard
Descend, and sit on each important card:
First *Ariel* perch'd upon a Matadore,
Then each, according to the rank they bore;
For *Sylphs*, yet mindful of their ancient race,
Are, as when women, wondrous fond of place.
Behold, four Kings in majesty rever'd,
With hoary whiskers and a forky beard;
And four fair Queens whose hands sustain a flow'r,
Th' expressive emblem of their softer pow'r;
Four Knaves in garbs succinct, a trusty band,
Caps on their heads, and halberts in their hand;

1. VER. 11. 12. Originally in the first edition,
In various talk the chearful hours they past,
Of, who was bitt, or who capotted last.

Hieher muß *Belindens* Boot seine stolzen Segel strecken,
Sie und jeder denkt allhier auch des Hofes Luft zu schmecken.
Mit erbaulichen Gesprächen wird die Zeit da hingebracht:
Wer den letzten Ball gegeben? oder den Besuch gemacht?
Einer rühmt die Königinn, die der Britten Inseln zieret;
Der beschreibt den Feuerschirm aus Sumatra hergeführet.
Einer deutet die Geberden, Blick und Minen, Wink und Sinn,
Und bey einem jeden Worte stirbt ein guter Namen hin.
Schnupftaback und Fächer dient, jede Pause von Geschwätzen,
Wie das Singen, Lachen, Wehn, und das Aeugeln, zu ersetzen.

Unterdessen wich die Sonne von dem Mittagshimmel ab,
Und schoß ihres Feuers Ausfluß schon mit schieferm Stral herab.
Richter, die der Hunger quält, unterschrieben ihr Ermessen;
Und der Dieb gieng schnell zum Strick; denn die Richter mußten essen.
Jeder Kaufmann ließ die Börse, und gieng ruhig in sein Haus,
Und des Putzens lange Mühe war beym Nachttisch endlich aus.

Ruhm und Ehrsucht treibt die Brust unsrer feurigen *Belinden*,
Zweene Ritter voller Muth zum Scharmützel auszufinden.
Aus dem schönen *Lomberspiele*[1] will sie ihr Verhängniß sehn;
Und wird stolz von einem Siege, der erst künftig soll geschehn.
Die geweihte neunte Zahl nahet sich in drey Schwadronen,
Steht in engen Gliedern da, rüstig, keinen Feind zu schonen.
Kaum beweget sie die Hände, so erscheint der Sylphen Schaar,
Lagert sich, und nimmt mit Sorgfalt jeder theuren Karte wahr.
Ariel nahm seinen Platz oben bey den Matadoren;
Wie die andern Stell und Ort sich nach ihrem Rang erkohren.
Denn die *Sylphen* sind noch immer, (diese Neigung stirbet nicht!)
Wie sie sonst als Weiber waren, eifrig auf den Rang erpicht.

Vier Monarchen sieht man hier majestätisch ausgeputzet,
Deren grauer Knäbelbart und gespaltner Stutzbart stutzet;
Nebst vier schönen Königinnen; deren Blumen in der Hand
Machen ihre sanftern Kräfte durch ein eignes Bild bekannt.
Mit den Mützen auf dem Kopf, Hellebarten in den Händen,
Sieht man noch vier Knechte sich aufgeschürzt zum Kampfe wenden:

1. Wer hier das Original nicht zu Rathe zieht, der wird aus der französischen Uebersetzung dieser Stelle schwerlich klug werden können. Es hat dem Verfasser derselben nicht gefallen, ausdrücklich das Lomberspiel zu nennen, wie Pope thut: und drum weis man nicht eher, wovon die Rede ist, als bis er die Matadore nennet. Die Zeile aber

And swells her breast with conquests yet to come,

heißt gar nicht: 'son air triomphant annonce sa victoire prochaine', *ihre siegende Miene zeiget ihren bevorstehenden Sieg an*. Im Englischen ist es ein feiner Spott über Leute, die sich auf noch ungewisse Sachen schon viel zu gute thun.

And particolour'd troops, a shining train,
Draw forth to combat on the velvet plain.
The skilful Nymph reviews her force with care:
Let Spades be trumps! she said, and trumps they were.
Now move to war her sable Matadores,
In show like leaders of the swarthy Moors.
Spadillio first, unconquerable Lord!
Led off two captive trumps, and swept the board.
As many more *Manillio* forc'd to yield,
And march'd a victor from the verdant field.
Him *Basto* follow'd, but his fate more hard
Gain'd but one trump and one *Plebeian* card.
With his broad sabre next, a chief in years,
The hoary Majesty of Spades appears,
Puts forth one manly leg, to fight reveal'd,
The rest, his many-colour'd robe conceal'd.
The rebel Knave, who dares his prince engage,
Proves the just victim of his royal rage.
Ev'n mighty *Pam*, that Kings and Queens o'erthrew,
And mow'd down armies in the fights of *Lu*,
Sad chance of war! now destitute of aid,
Falls undistinguish'd by the victor Spade!
Thus far both armies to *Belinda* yield;
Now to the Baron fate inclines the field.
His warlike *Amazon* her host invades,
Th' imperial consort of the crown of Spades.
The Club's black Tyrant first her victim dy'd,
Spite of his haughty mien, and barb'rous pride:
What boots the regal circle on his head,
His giant limbs, in state unwieldy spread;
That long behind he trails his pompous robe,
And, of all monarchs, only grasps the globe?
The Baron now his Diamonds pours apace;
Th' embroider'd King who shows but half his face,
And his refulgent Queen, with pow'rs combin'd,
Of broken troops an easy conquest find.
Clubs, Diamonds, Hearts, in wild disorder seen,
With throngs promiscuous strow the level green.
Thus when dispers'd a routed army runs,
Of *Asia's* troops, and *Afric's* sable sons,
With like confusion different nations fly,
Of various habit, and of various dye,

Und ein Heer von zwoen Farben, das mit wundervollem Staat
Vorwärts rückt, und sich dem Streite auf dem sammtnen Boden naht.
Nunmehr stellt die Nymphe schon ihre Schaaren, mit den Worten:
Pick sey Trumpf! und Pick war Trumpf. Nun ist Streit an allen Orten!
Durch die schwarzen Matadore fängt der Krieg am ersten an;
Wie man bey den braunen Mohren ihre Führer schauen kann.
Erstlich hat *Spadille* sich, die noch niemand überwunden,
Mit zween Trümpfen, die sie schlug, bey der Schönen eingefunden.
Eben so viel schlägt *Manille*, fast in einem Augenblick,
Und kömmt von dem grünen Felde stolz, als Siegerinn, zurück.
Basta folgt, doch das Geschick läßt sie nicht so viel erlangen:
Sie bekömmt nur einen Trumpf, und ein Pöbelblatt gefangen.
Schaut des Aeltesten von allen ungeheure Majestät!
Den *Pickkönig*, der zum Kampfe mit dem breiten Säbel geht;
Der nur einen Fuß entblößt, und denselben vor sich strecket,
Weil des andern Körpers Theil sein buntscheckigt Kleid bedecket.
Der rebellische *Pickbube*, der dem Fürsten trotzen darf,
Wird sein Opfer, und empfindet seines Königs Rache scharf.
Treffelknecht, der sonsten wohl Könige nebst Königinnen
Im Scherwenzel überwand, kann doch dießmal nicht entrinnen;
Sondern muß, o Glück des Krieges! weil kein Freund ihm bey will stehn,
Als ein unbekannter Kriegsknecht, durch den Sieger untergehn.
Beyde Heere mußten so noch bisher *Belinden* weichen:
Doch nunmehr giebt das Geschick dem *Baron* ein günstig Zeichen.
Die bewehrte Amazoninn greift den Feind recht muthig an,
Und zeigt bald, was die Gemahlinn des *Pickkönigs* wirken kann.
Treffels schwarzer Wüterich muß zuerst ihr Opfer werden,
Trotz dem ungeschlachten Stolz, und den grimmigen Geberden.
Wozu dient die Königskrone, die sein gräulich Haupt bedeckt?
Seine plumpen Riesenglieder, die er tölpisch ausgestreckt?
Wozu dient ihm nun der Schweif, den sein langer Mantel schleifet;
Und der Weltkreis in der Hand, den sonst kein Monarch ergreifet?
Jetzo wird der *Careauhaufen* dem Baron zur Schlacht geneigt,
Dessen reichbebrämter König nur sein halbes Antlitz zeigt.
Die geputzte Königinn sammlet die zerstreuten Schaaren,
Kömmt, und schlägt, und kann allhier einen leichten Sieg erfahren.
Hier erblickt man *Careau*, *Treffel*, *Coeur* und alles ganz zerstreut,
Wie es dick in bunten Schaaren, Feld und Wahlstatt überkleidt.
Wie ein Asiaterheer und die Africaner ziehen,
Wenn sie ganz zerstreuet sind, und in wilden Haufen fliehen.
Mit gleich schrecklicher Verwirrung sieht man ganze Völker ziehn,
Und in ganz verschiednen Kleidern und verschiedner Farbe fliehn.

The pierc'd battalions dis-united fall,
In heaps on heaps; one fate o'erwhelms them all.
        The Knave of Diamonds tries his wily arts,
And wins (oh shameful chance!) the Queen of Hearts.
At this, the blood the virgin's cheek forsook,
A livid paleness spreads o'er all her look;
She sees, and trembles at th' approaching ill,
Just in the jaws of ruin, and *Codille.*
And now, (as oft' in some distemper'd State)
On one nice Trick depends the gen'ral fate.
An Ace of Hearts steps forth: The King unseen
Lurk'd in her hand, and mourn'd his captive Queen:
He springs to vengeance with an eager pace,
And falls like thunder on the prostrate Ace.
The nymph exulting fills with shouts the sky;
The walls, the woods, and long canals reply.
        Oh thoughtless mortals! ever blind to fate,
Too soon dejected, and too soon elate.
Sudden, these honours shall be snatch'd away,
And curs'd for ever this victorious day.
        For lo! the board with cups and spoons is crown'd,
The berries crackle, and the mill turns round;
On shining Altars of *Japan* they raise
The silver lamp; the fiery spirits blaze:
From silver spouts the grateful liquors glide,
While *China's* earth receives the smoaking tyde:
At once they gratify their scent and taste,
And frequent cups prolong the rich repaste.
Strait hover round the Fair her airy band;
Some, as she sipp'd, the fuming liquor fann'd,
Some o'er her lap their careful plumes display'd,
Trembling, and conscious of the rich brocade.
Coffee, (which makes the politician wise,
And see thro' all things with his half-shut eyes)
Sent up in vapours to the Baron's brain

Die getrennte Kriegesschaar naht sich hier zugleich dem Falle,
Haufen liegt bey Haufen da, und ein Schicksal trifft sie alle.
Der verschmitzte *Careaubube* naht sich auch mit keckem Sinn,
Und (o schimpferfüllter Zufall!) schlägt der Herzen Königinn.
Hier verläßt das frische Blut auf einmal *Belindens* Wangen:
Sie erblaßt, daß sich das Glück so zu ändern angefangen.
Sie erschrickt und zittert heftig, vor der nah vorhandnen Noth,
In dem Rachen des Verlustes, der ihr die *Codille* droht.
Nun beruhts, (so wie es oft in verwirrten Staaten[1] gehet,)
Nur auf einer Kleinigkeit, wie das ganze Schicksal stehet.
Herzendaus kömmt angezogen; dessen König, ganz bewegt,
In *Belindens* Händen traurte, daß man sein Gemahl erlegt.
Gleich dem Donner eilt er zu, Sieg und Rache zu genießen,
Und das *Daus* muß sein Vergehn mit dem härtsten Falle büssen.
Hier frohlockete die Nymphe, durch ein helles Lustgeschrey:
Wände, Wälder, Thal und Flüsse stimmten ihrem Jauchzen bey.
Schwacher und verblendter Mensch! jedes Glück macht dich verwegen,
Jeder Unglücksfall verzagt. Bald wird sich der Hochmuth legen!
Bald verschwindet diese Freude, dieser Ehre leerer Schein,
Und der Tag, so reich an Siegen, wird der Nachwelt Schrecken seyn.
Nunmehr bringt der Caffeetisch Löffelchen und Caffeeschalen:
Die gebrannte Bohne knirscht, die die kleinen Mühlen mahlen.
Man errichtet die Altäre, wie man sie in *Japan* kennt,
Und die schweren Silberlampen, drinn der blaue Weingeist brennt.
Aus der silbern Wasserkunst muß der schöne Trank jetzt fließen,
Und die heiße Ebb und Fluth sich in Japans Thon ergießen.
Der Geschmack und auch das Riechen wird zu gleicher Zeit ergetzt,
Und durch immer neue Schälchen die Erfrischung fortgesetzt:
Da *Belindens Sylphenwacht* dicht zu ihrem Schutze stehet,
Ihr, indem sie trinkt, den Dampf des Caffees zum Kühlen wehet;
Oder die getreuen Flügel über ihren Schooß erstreckt,
Und mit tausend Furcht und Zittern den brokadnen Rock bedeckt.
Der Caffee, der oftermals eines Staatsmanns Geist erbauet,
Daß sein halbgeschloßner Blick schwere Sachen durchgeschauet;
Hilft anjetzt durch seine Dünste dem *Baron* zu neuer List,

1. Im Originale steht 'distemper'd State', und es habe nun Herr Pope entweder die damalige Verfassung des französischen oder brittischen Hofes damit im Sinne gehabt; so sieht man wohl, daß es eine Leichtfertigkeit von ihm ist. Der französische Dollmetscher aber ist so gut, und macht 'des cas extrêmes' daraus. Ob hieran eine große politische Behutsamkeit schuld seyn soll, die gleichwohl Herrn Popen auch eingefallen wäre, wenn sie hier erforderlich gewesen; oder ob es nur die gewöhnliche Nachläßigkeit der franz. Uebersetzer englischer Originale so mit sich gebracht, das weis ich nicht. Genug, Pope sagt ganz was anders, als sein ungetreuer Uebersetzer ihn sagen läßt.

New stratagems, the radiant Lock to gain.
Ah cease, rash youth! desist e'er 'tis too late,
Fear the just Gods, and think of *Scylla's* Fate![1]
Chang'd to a bird, and sent to flit in air,
She dearly pays for *Nisus'* injur'd hair!
But when to mischief mortals bend their will,
How soon they find fit instruments of ill?
Just then, *Clarissa* drew with tempting grace
A two-edg'd weapon from her shining case;
So Ladies in Romance assist their Knight,
Present the spear, and arm him for the fight.
He takes the gift with rev'rence, and extends
The little engine on his finger's ends;
This just behind *Belinda's* neck he spread,
As o'er the fragrant steams she bends her head.
Swift to the Lock a thousand Sprites repair,
A thousand wings, by turns, blow back the hair;
And thrice they twitch'd the diamond in her ear;
Thrice she look'd back, and thrice the foe drew near.
Just in that instant, anxious *Ariel* sought
The close recesses of the Virgin's thought;
As on the nosegay in her breast reclin'd,
He watch'd th' Ideas rising in her mind,
Sudden he view'd, in spite of all her art,
An earthly Lover lurking at her heart.
Amaz'd, confus'd, he found his pow'r expir'd,
Resign'd to fate, and with a sigh retir'd.

1. *Vide* Ovid. Metam. 8.

Wie er zu der Locke komme, die so schön und trefflich ist.
Frecher Jüngling! weiche doch, weils noch Zeit ist: weich zurücke!
Scheue doch der Götter Zorn! und der *Scylla* hart Geschicke!
Im Gefieder einer Lerche büßt sie in der Luft die That,
Die sie an des *Nisus* Haaren[1] frevelhaft begangen hat.
Aber wenn ein Sterblicher sich zur Bosheit will verbinden,
Wird er leicht zu seinem Zweck auch geschickte Mittel finden.
Schaut! *Clarice* zieht voll Anmuth aus dem blanken Futteral,
Gleichsam zu des Ritters Reizung, einen zweygespitzten Stahl.
So gehts bey Turnieren zu, wo die Ritter mit den Speeren,
Aus der Schönen eignen Hand, rüstig zum Gefechte kehren.
Ehrfurchtsvoll nimmt er die Gabe, wie man leicht vermuthen kann,
Und greift dieß geschliffne Werkzeug mit der Finger Spitzen an.
Und indem die Schöne sich nach dem Caffeedampf will bücken,
Oeffnet er den Zwillingstahl unvermerkt an ihrem Rücken.
Plötzlich kömmt ein Heer von Geistern, dem nicht wohl zu Muthe war:
Tausend Flügel wechselsweise flattern um ihr lockicht Haar.
Dreymal zupfen sie bestürzt ihren Ohrschmuck auf und nieder,
Dreymal sah sie sich herum; dreymal kam der Feind auch wieder.
In demselben Augenblicke[2] war ihr Schutzgeist voller Leid,
Und durchspürt, mit vielem Eifer, ihres Sinnes Heimlichkeit:
Als er sich an ihrer Brust in den Blumenstraus gemachet,
Und mit Eifer jedes Bild ihres Herzens scharf bewachet.
Plötzlich sah er ganz bestürzt, was ihm keine Kunst verdeckte,
Daß ein Buhler irrdscher Art in der Schönen Herzen steckte;
Merkt das Ende seines Schutzes: er erstaunet und erbleicht,
Giebt sich in des Schicksals Willen, seufzt vor Wehmuth und entweicht.

1. Minos belagerte die Stadt Megara, und konnte sie nicht bezwingen, weil das Glück oder Unglück dieses Reiches darinnen bestund, daß ihr König Nisus unter seinen grauen Haaren ein einziges purpurrothes Haar hatte: so lange er aber dieß behielt, war er unüberwindlich. Seine Tochter Scylla nun, die sich in den König Minos verliebt hatte, und der das Geheimniß bekannt war, schnitt ihrem Vater dieses Haar ab, und brachte es dem Minos. Darüber ward sie zu einer Lerche. *Ouid. Metam. VIII.*
2. Bey diesem ganzen Absatze hat der französische Uebersetzer sich selbst übertroffen, und ein rechtes Meisterstück einer verstümmelten und falschen Uebersetzung gemacht. Er sagt: 'Le vigilant Ariel voulut penetrer sa pensée; mais helas! tout son art ne lui servit alors, qu'à decouvrir un terrestre Amour caché dans le coeur de Baron'. *Der wachsame Ariel wollte ihre Gedanken errathen* (so kurz und körnicht wird der Uebersetzer mit den vier Versen seines Originals fertig: der Blumenstraus, darinnen der Sylphe gelauert, und alles, ist da schon mit drinnen) *aber ach! alle seine Kunst half ihm damals nichts mehr, als daß er in des Barons Herzen eine irrdische Liebe wahrnahm*. So schön hat er die Zeilen verstanden:

   Sudden he view'd, in spite of all her *art,*
   An earthly Lover lurking at her *heart.*

The Peer now spreads the glitt'ring *Forfex* wide,
T' inclose the Lock; now joins it, to divide.
Ev'n then, before the fatal engine clos'd,
A wretched *Sylph* too fondly interpos'd;
Fate urg'd the sheers, and cut the *Sylph* in twain,
(But airy substance soon unites again)[1]
The meeting points the sacred hair dissever
From the fair head, for ever, and for ever!

Then flash'd the living lightning from her eyes,
And screams of horror rend th' affrighted skies.
Not louder shrieks to pitying heav'n are cast,
When husbands or when lapdogs breathe their last;
Or when rich *China* vessels fall'n from high,
In glitt'ring dust, and painted fragments lie!

Let wreaths of triumph now my temples twine,
(The Victor cry'd) the glorious Prize is mine!
While fish in streams, or birds delight in air,
Or in a Coach and six the *British* Fair,
As long as *Atalantis* shall be read,
Or the small pillow grace a Lady's bed,
While visits shall be paid on solemn days,
When num'rous wax-lights in bright order blaze,
While nymphs take treats, or assignations give,
So long my honour, name, and praise shall live!

What Time wou'd spare, from Steel receives its date,
And monuments, like men, submit to fate!
Steel could the labour of the Gods destroy,
And strike to dust th' imperial tow'rs of *Troy*;
Steel could the works of mortal pride confound,
And hew triumphal arches to the ground.
What wonder then, fair nymph! thy hairs shou'd feel
The conqu'ring force of unresisted steel?

1. *See* Milton, *lib.* 6 *of* Satan *cut asunder by the Angel* Michael.

Nunmehr sieht man den Baron seine Spitzen offen halten,
Um *Belindens* schönes Haar erst zu fassen, dann zu spalten.
Eh sich aber das Gelenke des ergrimmten Stahles schließt,
Wagt ein *Sylphe* sich darzwischen, der zu zärtlich sorgsam ist.
Das Verhängniß schließt den Stahl, und der *Sylphe* wird zertheilet;
(Aber Wesen luftger Art[1] sind gleich wiederum geheilet,)
Bis die göttergleiche Locke, durch der beyden Spitzen Schluß,
Sich vom schönen Kopf auf immer und auf ewig trennen muß.
Schaut den zornerfüllten Blitz aus *Belindens* Augen dringen!
Hört das grimmige Getös in erschrocknen Lüften klingen!
Kein Geschrey zum milden Himmel hat man noch so stark gespürt,
Wenn der Tod wo einen Ehmann oder Schooßhund abgeführt;
Oder wenn ein Porcellan von der Höh herunter fället,
Daß die reichgemalte Pracht an dem Boden sich zerschellet.
„Nunmehr müssen Siegeskränze meiner Stirne Zierath seyn!
(Rief der hocherfreute Sieger:) „dieser schöne Preis ist mein!
„Weil die Fische noch im Strom, Vögel in den Lüften wallen,
„Und in stolzen Kutschen sich Englands Schönen wohlgefallen;
„Weil der *Atalantis* Mährchen noch der Leser Herzen rührt,
„Und ein schmales Tassentküssen unsrer Nymphen Bette ziert;
„Weil an Gallatagen man noch Besuche wird empfangen,
„Wo der Kerzen große Zahl pflegt mit seltnem Glanz zu prangen;
„Weil die Nymphen noch gern tanzen, weil sie noch die Liebe plagt,
„Wird mir bey der späten Nachwelt Ruhm und Ehre nachgesagt."
Was die strenge Zeit verschont, unterwirft der Stahl dem Falle;
Mensch und Denkmaal zeigen dieß: ein Verhängniß trifft sie alle!
Hat der Götter eigne Werke nicht der Stahl zu Fall gebracht;
Und auch *Trojens* Königsthürme endlich noch zu Schutt gemacht?
Stahl vernichtet jedes Werk, was der Menschen Stolz errichtet:
Sind die Siegesbögen selbst nicht durch seine Macht vernichtet?
Ists denn Wunder, schöne Nymphe! daß des Stahles strenge Wuth
An dem Schmucke deiner Haare die gewohnte Wirkung thut?

Ende des dritten Buches.

1. Herr Pope ist so leichtfertig, daß er hier Miltons VI Buch des *verlohrnen Paradieses* anzieht, allwo der Engel Michael den Satan mitten von einander schneidet. Er hätte aber diesen Gewährsmann nicht gebraucht: denn was in einem scherzhaften Gedichte die Lustigkeit des Lesers vermehret, das ist in einem Heldengedichte, wo man von nichts minderm handelt, als von dem allgemeinen Unglücke des ganzen menschlichen Geschlechts, ungeheuer und unsinnig. Sylphen und Stutzer können wohl Spaß treiben: sie werden lächerlich, und ein mehrers bringt ihre Natur nicht mit sich. Aber wenn der Engel Michael und Satan mit einander solche Possen treiben, daß sie sich in Stücken schneiden, und gleich wieder zusammen wachsen; so muß man am Verstande so blind seyn, wie Milton an den Augen war, wofern man dergleichen Brocken bewundern will.

Canto IV.

But anxious cares the pensive nymph oppress'd,[1]
And secret passions labour'd in her breast.
Not youthful kings in battle seiz'd alive,
Not scornful virgins who their charms survive,
Not ardent lovers robb'd of all their bliss,
Not ancient ladies when refus'd a kiss,
Not tyrants fierce that unrepenting die,
Not *Cynthia* when her manteau's pinn'd awry,
E'er felt such rage, resentment and despair,
As thou, sad Virgin! for thy ravish'd Hair.
For, that sad moment when the·*Sylphs* withdrew,
And *Ariel* weeping from *Belinda* flew,
Umbriel, a dusky, melancholy sprite,
As ever sully'd the fair face of light,
Down to the central earth, his proper scene,
Repair'd to search the gloomy Cave of *Spleen*.
Swift on his sooty pinions flits the *Gnome*,
And in a vapour reach'd the dismal dome.
No chearful breeze this sullen region knows,
The dreaded East is all the wind that blows.
Here in a grotto, shelter'd close from air,
And screen'd in shades from day's detested glare,
She sighs for ever on her pensive bed,
Pain at her side, and *Megrim* at her head.
Two handmaids wait the throne: alike in place,
But diff'ring far in figure and in face.
Here stood *Ill-nature* like an ancient maid,
Her wrinkled form in black and white array'd;
With store of pray'rs, for mornings, nights, and noons,
Her hand is fill'd; her bosom with lampoons.
There *Affectation*, with a sickly mien,
Shows in her cheek the roses of eighteen,
Practis'd to lisp, and hang the head aside,
Faints into airs, and languishes with pride,
On the rich quilt sinks with becoming woe,
Wrapt in a gown, for sickness, and for show.
The fair-ones feel such maladies as these,
When each new night-dress gives a new disease.

1. VER. I. Virg. Æn. 4. *At regina gravi, &c*. VOL. I.

Das vierte Buch.

Aber Sorgen, Gram und Kummer stören unsrer Nymphe Lust,
Und geheime Leidenschaften martern die bestürmte Brust.
Nein, so raast kein junger Prinz, den man in der Schlacht gefangen;
Keine Spröde zürnet so, der der Jugend Reiz vergangen;
Kein erhitzt verliebter Buhler, den ein schmerzlich Unglück plagt;
Keine hochbejahrte Jungfer, der man einen Kuß versagt;
Auch kein Wütrich sonder Reu, den sein nahes Ende schrecket;
Selber *Chloris*, der die Magd ihren Anputz schief gestecket,
Fühlt dergleichen Rasereyen, Rachgier und Verzweiflung nicht,
Als dich, aufgebrachtes Fräulein, um der Locke Raub anficht.
Denn denselben Augenblick, als die *Sylphen* sie verließen,
Und ihr treuer *Ariel* fast in Thränen wollt zerfließen,
Senkte sich ein finstrer *Gnome*, *Umbriel*, der Poltergeist,
Der des heitern Sonnenlichtes ärgster Schimpf und Schandfleck heißt,
Zu der Erden Mittelpunkt, wo er recht nach Würden wohnet,
Und begab sich in die Kluft, wo die trübe *Milzsucht* thronet.
Auf den schwarzberußten Schwingen schwebt der schnelle *Gnome* fort,
Und erreicht in trübem Dampfe ihren grauserfüllten Ort.
Diese Kluft kennt nicht den Hauch unsrer lieblichen Zephiren;
Nur des Ostwinds rauhe Wuth läßt sich hier mit Schrecken spüren.
Allhier seufzt in einer Grotte, wo kein Lüftchen Eingang findt,
Und des Tages heitrer Schimmer in verwünschten Schatten schwindt,
Diese Göttinn, die voll Harm auf dem Grillenbette lieget,
Der zur Seiten sich die *Pein*, und ans Haupt das *Kopfweh* füget.
Zwo getreue Kammermädchen, von verschiedener Gestalt,
Haben, gleich an Rang und Würde, neben ihr den Aufenthalt.
Mit verschrumpftem Angesicht läßt sich hier die *Bosheit* blicken,
Ihrer Kleider Putz besteht aus halb weiß halb schwarzen Stücken.
Früh, des Morgens, auch des Mittags, ja bey später Eulenflucht,
Füllt der *Cubach* ihr die Hände, und das Herz die Lästersucht.
Die *Verstellung* sieht man dort, die sich krank zu seyn bemühet,
Obgleich ihrer Wangen Pracht von der Jugend Rosen blühet.
Uebt sich im gezwungnen Lispeln, hängt den Kopf zur Seiten hin,
Fällt in Ohnmacht, sich zu zieren, und thut matt, aus stolzem Sinn;
Sinket auf den reichen Pfühl, mit anmuthigem Erblassen,
In ein Nachtkleid eingehüllt, Putz und Krankheit sehn zu lassen:
Wie es unsre Schönen machen, denen es durch List gelingt,
Daß ein jeder neuer Nachtputz eine neue Krankheit bringt.

A constant Vapour o'er the palace flies;
Strange phantoms rising as the mists arise;
Dreadful, as hermit's dreams in haunted shades,
Or bright, as visions of expiring maids.
Now glaring fiends, and snakes on rolling spires,
Pale spectres, gaping tombs, and purple fires:
Now lakes of liquid gold, *Elysian* scenes,
And crystal domes, and Angels in machines.
Unnumber'd throngs on ev'ry side are seen,
Of bodies chang'd to various forms by Spleen.
Here living Tea-pots stand, one arm held out,
One bent; the handle this, and that the spout:
A Pipkin there, like *Homer's* Tripod walks;[1]

1. *See* Hom. *Illiad* 18. *of* Vulcan's *walking Tripods.*

Ein beständig dicker Dunst hält hier den Palast bedecket,
Dessen trüber Nebelduft seltsame Gestalten hecket:
Schrecklich, wie sich ein Cartheuser träumend in den Wüsten härmt;
Oder lieblich, wie im Sterben eine junge Schöne schwärmt.
Hier sind Feinde voller Glut, Schlangen mit gekrümmten Rücken,
Blasse Schatten, Purpurfeur, offne Gräber zu erblicken:
Dort ein See geschmolznes Goldes, manches Stück Eliserfeld,
Ganze Tempel von Crystallen, Engel aus der Opernwelt.
Ganze Haufen sieht man hier sich aus allen Ecken dringen,
Von den Leibern, die die Milz konnt in andre Formen bringen.
Mancher Theetopf steht und lebet, strecket einen Arm empor,
Setzt den andern in die Seite; jens die Pfeife, dieß das Ohr.
Wie den *Dreyfuß* beym *Homer*[1] sieht man hier ein Töpfchen gehen,

1. Homer schreibt im XVIII Buche der Ilias, daß, da die Thetis den Vulcan besuchet, um ihn zu bitten, daß er für ihren Sohn, den Achilles, dessen Waffen durch den Tod des Patroklus, seines Freundes, in Hektors Hände gefallen waren, andre verfertigen möchte; sie denselben bey Verfertigung 20 goldner Stühle angetroffen, die zu einem prächtigen Palaste kommen sollten, und so gemacht waren, daß sie von selbst in die Versammlungen gehen, und sich wieder an Ort und Stelle zurück begeben könnten. Julius Scaliger hat nach seiner gewöhnlichen Art, sich über diese Stelle im Homer sehr lustig gemacht, und gemeynt: 'Wenn Vulkan hier hätte Stühle machen können, die von sich selbst giengen, warum er nicht auch Töpfe gemacht hätte, die das Fleisch von selbst gekocht hätten?' Wenn man dem guten Scaliger eben so scharfsinnig hätte antworten wollen; so hätte man nur sagen dörfen: Vulkan sey kein Töpfer gewesen, oder habe nicht für die holländischen Gelehrten gearbeitet, bey denen das Holz so theuer ist. Allein Herr Dacier vertheidiget den Homer dergestalt; er schreibt: 'Wenn man den Dichtern Schuld giebt, sie hätten etwas unmögliches vorgebracht, so muß man diese Unmöglichkeit 1) im Absehen auf die Poesie, 2) im Absehen auf das, was besser ist, und 3) im Absehen auf den Ruf, betrachten'. Nach allen diesen drey Stücken nun vertheidiget er den Homer. Denn er zeigt 1) daß das Heldengedicht dergleichen Unmöglichkeit eben begehre, und sie sogar bis auf das Unvernünftige hinaustreibe; nur so, daß die *Wahrscheinlichkeit* dabey nicht beleidiget werde. 2) Daß die Sache auf diese Art seltsamer und vortrefflicher werde, und das Original einer Sache immer die Oberhand behalten müsse. 3) Daß er auch dem Rufe gefolget sey, der den Göttern die Allmacht zugestund. (Siehe der Frau Dacier Uebersetzung der Ilias, im 3 Th. 118 Seite, Amsterd. Ausg. von 1731.) Ich glaube nicht, daß jemanden hier wiederum Miltons Teufel einfallen sollte, den der Michael entzwey geschnitten; als wenn näml. auch dieser Dichter auf obige Weise zu rechtfertigen wäre. Denn eben nach diesen drey Regeln taugt diese ganze Erfindung nicht. Nach der 1) nicht: denn sie ist zwar *bis aufs Unvernünftige hinausgetrieben*; allein wie ist es *wahrscheinlich*, daß ein Geist den andern zerhauen könne? 2) Ist die Sache auch nicht besser, und giebt dem Leser keinen höhern Begriff vom Engel Michael; denn seines gleichen in Stücken hauen, das thun die Husaren und Panduren alle Tage. 3) Hat Milton auch den Ruf nicht für sich: denn niemand hat noch den Engeln oder Teufeln eine unumschränkte Gewalt über einander zugestanden, so daß sie sich nach Gefallen aus dem Wege räumen könnten. Diese Macht steht dem höchsten Wesen allein zu. Hierzu könnte man noch meines wenigen Bedünkens setzen, daß 4) auch eine größere Ehre für den Urheber solcher wunderwürdigen Kunststücke, aus der Erdichtung fließen muß, wenn nämlich ihm sein Kunststück gelingt.

Here sighs a Jar, and there a Goose-pye talks;[1]
Men prove with child, as pow'rful fancy works,
And maids turn'd bottles, call aloud for corks.
Safe past the *Gnome* thro' this fantastic band,
A branch of healing Spleenwort in his hand.
Then thus address'd the pow'r — Hail wayward Queen!
Who rule the sex to fifty from fifteen:
Parent of vapours and of female wit,
Who give th' hysteric, or poetic fit,
On various tempers act by various ways,
Make some take physic, others scribble plays;
Who cause the proud their visits to delay,
And send the godly in a pett, to pray.
A nymph there is, that all thy pow'r disdains,
And thousands more in equal mirth maintains.
But oh! if e'er thy *Gnome* could spoil a grace,
Or raise a pimple on a beauteous face,
Like Citron-waters matrons cheeks inflame,
Or change complexions at a losing game;
If e'er with airy horns I planted heads,
Or rumpled petticoats, or tumbled beds,
Or caus'd suspicion when no soul was rude,
Or discompos'd the head-dress of a Prude,
Or o'er to costive lap-dog gave disease,
Which not the tears of brightest eyes could ease:
Hear me, and touch *Belinda* with chagrin;
That single act gives half the world the spleen.
The Goddess with a discontented air
Seems to reject him, tho' she grants his pray'r.
A wond'rous Bag with both her hands she binds,
Like that where once *Ulysses* held the winds;

1. Alludes to a real fact, a Lady of distinction imagin'd herself in this condition.

Ganspasteten schwatzen hier, und die Trinkgeschirre flehen.
Mannspersonen werden schwanger, die die Phantasie bethört,
Und die Mädchen werden Gläser, die man deutlich ächzen hört.
Unser *Gnome* kömmt beglückt durch dieß Herr der Phantaseyen,
Milzkraut trägt er in der Hand, die Gespenster zu zerstreuen.
Naht zum Thron mit diesen Worten: „Sey, o Göttinn, mir gegrüßt,
„Die von funfzehn bis an funfzig unsrer Schönen Leitstern ist.
„O du Quell der Mutterpein, und des Witzes unsrer Schönen!
„Die du theils hysterisch machst, theils zum Dichten kannst gewöhnen.
„Deren Kraft verschiedne Seelen durch verschiedne Wege treibt,
„Daß die eine Pillen schlucket, diese schlechte Verse schreibt;
„Die du eine Spröde treibst, daß sie den Besuch verschiebet,
„Und die Fromme, daß sie sich zum Gebeth im Zorn begiebet.
„Eine Nymphe lebt auf Erden, welche deine Macht verhöhnt,
„Und noch tausend andre Seelen zu vergnügter Lust verwöhnt.
„Aber, hat dein treuer *Gnom* jemals einen Reiz entwendet,
„Und durch Finnen und Geschwür je ein schön Gesicht geschändet;
„Oder je Matronenwangen mit Citronengelb beschmiert;
„Oder bey verlohrnem Spiele schöner Wangen Roth entführt[1];
„Je ein eingebildet Horn auf der Männer Stirn gerücket;
„Einen Unterrock zerzaust, oder Betten eingedrücket;
„Einen Argwohn oft erreget, wenn kein Mensch daran gedacht;
„Oder einer Spröden Kopfputz aus dem Ebenmaaß gebracht;
„Dem verstopften Schooßhund oft eine Schwachheit eingegeben,
„Die der schönsten Augen Paar nicht durch Thränen konnte heben:
„Göttinn! o so hör mein Flehen; mach *Belinden* misvergnügt!
„Dieß allein macht, daß die Hälfte dieser Welt die Milzsucht kriegt.
Ein verdrußerfüllter Blick, den die Göttinn zu ihm kehret,
Zeiget, sie versag ihm das, was sie gleichwohl ihm gewähret.
Sie ergreift mit beyden Händen einen Schlauch von seltner Art,
Wie der Windschlauch des *Ulysses*; in demselben wird bewahrt

Und beym Homer gelingts dem Vulkan: seine Stühle gehen wirklich. Miltons Michael aber besteht mit Schanden; der zerhauene Teufel wächst gleich wieder zusammen. Dieses kann ihm nun zwar niemand übel nehmen: aber warum hat denn der Engel zugehauen, wenn er wußte, daß er nichts davon gebessert seyn würde? Man lacht ihn also mit seiner mislungenen Helden- und Staatsaction aus; so wie hier der Baron ausgelacht wird.

1. Diese Zeile fehlt in der französischen Uebersetzung ganz und gar; jedoch ich bin es überdrüßig, ihre Schnitzer ferner aufzusuchen, sonst würde ich a. d. 29 Seite schon erinnert haben, daß daselbst die 9 und 10 Zeile, 'Schrecklich, wie sich ein Cartheuser & c.' von dem gallischen Uebersetzer ebenfalls unterdrückt worden sind [i.e. IV.41-42-H.B.], und daß er aus der *Pein*, die neben der Göttinn gestanden, *den Eigensinn*, 'Bisarrerie', aus den zwey Kammermädchen aber *zween Chöre von Mädchen*, 'deux Choeurs de filles' gemacht, und überhaupt fast im allen Absätzen den Pope verstümmelt und verdrehet hat.

There she collects the force of female lungs,
Sighs, sobs, and passions, and the war of tongues.
A Vial next she fills with fainting fears,
Soft sorrows, melting griefs, and flowing tears.
The *Gnome* rejoicing bears her gifts away,
Spreads his black wings, and slowly mounts to day.

Sunk in *Thalestris'* arms the nymph he found,
Her eyes dejected and her hair unbound.
Full o'er their heads the swelling bag he rent,
And all the Furies issued at the vent.
Belinda burns with more than mortal ire,
And fierce *Thalestris* fans the rising fire.
O wretched maid! she spread her hands, and cry'd,
(While *Hampton's* echoes, wretched maid! reply'd)
Was it for this you took such constant care
The bodkin, comb, and essence to prepare?
For this your locks in paper durance bound,
For this with tort'ring irons wreath'd around?
For this with fillets strain'd your tender head,
And bravely bore the double loads of lead?
Gods! shall the ravisher display your hair,
While the Fops envy, and the Ladies stare!
Honour forbid! at whose unrival'd shrine
Ease, pleasure, virtue, all our sex resign.
Methinks already I your tears survey,
Already hear the horrid things they say,
Already see you a degraded toast,
And all your honour in a whisper lost!
How shall I, then, your helpless fame defend?
'Twill then be infamy to seem your friend!
And shall this prize, th' inestimable prize,
Expos'd thro' crystal to the gazing eyes,
And heighten'd by the diamond's circling rays,
On that rapacious hand for ever blaze?
Sooner shall grass in *Hyde-park Circus* grow,
And wits take lodgings in the sound of *Bow*;
Sooner let earth, air, sea, to *Chaos* fall,
Men, monkeys, lap-dogs, parrots, perish all!

Und von ihr hinein gethan, alle Kraft der Weiberlungen,
Seufzer, Schluchzen, Zorn und Wuth, und der ganze Krieg der Zungen.
Dann erfüllt sie eine Flasche, und thut ebenfalls hinein:
Ohnmacht, Furcht, und zarte Schmerzen, Thränenbäche, Flehn und Schreyn.
Beydes trägt der *Gnome* fort, spreitet seine schwarzen Schwingen,
Und versuchet, dieß Geschenk in die Oberwelt zu bringen.
Mit geschlossnen nassen Augen, und mit aufgelöstem Haar,
Sah er, daß *Belinde* seufzend in *Thalestris* Armen war.
Hier zerreißt er seinen Schlauch oben über ihrem Haupte,
Welcher allen Furien nun den Ausgang frey erlaubte.
Ein fast mehr als menschlich Wüthen nimmt anitzt *Belinden* ein,
Und *Thalestris* will dem Feuer selbst ein neuer Zunder seyn.
„*Armes Kind*! so rief sie ans, mit empor geschwungnen Händen,
(*Hamptons* Echo rufet auch, *armes Kind*! von allen Wänden,)
„Ist es darum denn geschehen, daß du stets, mit Vorbedacht,
„Nadelküssen und Essenzen und den Kamm zurecht gemacht?
„Mußte darum nur dein Haar die papierne Marter fühlen?
„Und ein glüendes Metall deine Locken noch durchwühlen?
„Spannte darum das Geflechte deines zarten Kopfes Haut?
„Hat man darum an demselben ein gedoppelt Bley[1] geschaut?
„Himmel! soll des Räubers Hand mit der Locke pralen gehen,
„Wo die Stutzer neidisch sind, und die Schönen starre sehen?
„Dieß verbiethe doch die Ehre! gegen deren großen Werth
„Keine Schöne Vortheil, Tugend, oder andre Lust begehrt.
„Mich bedünkt, ich sehe schon deine Thränen und Geberden;
„Mich bedünkt, ich höre schon, was sie schrecklichs sagen werden.
„Ja, ich seh dich, schönen Abgott, schon von deinem Rang entehrt,
„Wie in einem tiefen Seufzer all dein Ruhm von dannen fährt.
„Ach! wie soll ich deinen Ruhm dann dem Untergang entreißen?
„Alsdann wird es schimpflich seyn, deine Freundinn noch zu heißen.
„Soll denn diese schöne Locke, dieser Locke Trefflichkeit
„Aller Augen auf sich ziehen, wenn sie ein Crystall bekleidt,
„Und der Diamanten Stral sie im Kreise wird umschließen,
„Noch an dieser Räuberfaust als ein Zierrath prangen müssen?
„Eher sollen Gras und Blumen in dem Hydepark entstehn,
„Und ein kluger Mensch da wohnen, wo die Stutzer schwärmen gehn!
„Eher mag doch Luft und See, und der ganze Ball der Erden,
„Mann, und Aff, und Papagey, Katz und Hund zum Chaos werden!

1. Um dieses zu verstehen, muß man sich auf die ehemalige Mode besinnen, da das Frauenzimmer unter den langen Haaren kleine Käppchen trug, die durch ein Band, an welchem in der Mitte unter dem Kinne zwey Bleygewichter hiengen, fest gemacht wurden, damit man die Haare glatt drüber aufschlagen und flechten konnte.

She said; then raging to Sir *Plume* repairs,
And bids her Beau demand the precious hairs:
(Sir *Plume*, of amber snuff-box justly vain,
And the nice conduct of a clouded cane)
With earnest eyes, and round unthinking face,
He first the snuff-box open'd, then the case,
And thus broke out — "My Lord, why, what the devil?
"Z–ds! damn the lock! 'fore Gad, you must be civil!
"Plague on't! 'tis past a jest — nay prithee, pox!
"Give her the hair" — he spoke, and rapp'd his box.
It grieves me much (reply'd the Peer again)
Who speaks so well should ever speak in vain.
But by this Lock, this sacred Lock I swear,[1]
(Which never more shall join its parted hair;
Which never more its honours shall renew,
Clip'd from the lovely head where late it grew)
That while my nostrils draw the vital air,
This hand which won it, shall for ever wear.
He spoke, and speaking, in proud triumph spread
The long-contended honours of her head.
But *Umbriel*, hateful *Gnome*! forbears not so;
He breaks the Vial whence the sorrows flow.
Then see! the nymph in beauteous grief appears,
Her eyes half-languishing, half-drown'd in tears;
On her heav'd bosom hung her drooping head,
Which, with a sigh, she rais'd; and thus she said.
For ever curs'd be this detested day,
Which snatch'd my best, my fav'rite curl away!
Happy! ah ten times happy had I been,
If *Hampton-Court* these eyes had never seen!
Yet am not I the first mistaken maid,
By love of Courts to num'rous ills betray'd.
Oh had I rather un-admir'd remain'd
In some lone isle, or distant Northern land;
Where the gilt Chariot never marks the way,
Where none learn *Ombre*, none e'er taste *Bohea*!
There kept my charms conceal'd from mortal eye,

1. *In allusion to* Achilles's *oath in* Homer. *Il.* I.

Dieses sagt sie, eilet plötzlich zu dem *Herrn von Feder* hin,
Und befiehlt ihm, jenem Freyherrn diese Locke zu entziehn.
Seines Stockes goldner Knopf, und des Bernsteins seltne Güte,
Der den Taback in sich schloß, bläheten sein stolz Gemüthe.
Mit gedankenleerer Stirne und mit rundem Angesicht
Oeffnet er zuerst die Dose; endlich bricht er aus und spricht:
„Was zum Teufel ist das, Lord ? — Hol der Henker doch die Haare!
„Ey du mußt auch höflich seyn! Daß dich! — die verwünschte Waare!
„Laß es gut seyn! — Nein! ich bitte, was ich immer bitten mag!
„Gieb mirs her!“ So sagt *Herr Feder*, und nimmt wiederum Taback.
Der *Baron* versetzt hierauf: „Traun, das Herze möcht mir brechen,
„Daß, wer so vortrefflich spricht, dennoch soll vergeblich sprechen.
„Aber bey der schönen Locke[1], bey der Locke schwör ich, Freund,
„Die kein Zufall künftig wieder mit dem schönen Kopf vereint;
„Und die ihren seltnen Schmuck niemals wird erneuert sehen,
„Da das schöne Haupt sie mißt, dessen Werth sie konnt erhöhen,
„Daß, so lange meine Nase noch den Othem ziehen kann,
„Diese Hand den Schmuck soll tragen, den sie voller List gewann.
Also sprach er, und zugleich hat er, was sein Arm errungen,
Das so lang' erwünschte Haar, trotzig durch die Luft geschwungen.
Umbrieln, dem bösen *Gnomen*, war auch dieß noch nicht genug;
Der die Flasche voller Sorgen plötzlich hier in Stücke schlug.
Nunmehr siehet man die *Nymph* in dem schönsten Schmerz erscheinen,
Ihre Blicke sind betrübt, und das Auge schmelzt vom Weinen:
Auf den aufgeblähten Busen senkt ihr mattes Haupt sich tief,
Das sie seufzend wieder aufhob, und zuletzt mit Aechzen rief:
„O vermaledeyter Tag! sey verfluchet und geschändet,
„Tag! an dem man mir mein Haar, meine liebste Lock entwendet!
„O wie selig könnt ich heißen! o wie wohl wär mir geschehn,
„Hätt ich doch mit diesen Augen *Hampton* nimmermehr gesehn!
„Doch, ich bin die erste nicht, die des Hofes Lustbarkeiten,
„Wenn sie sich darein vergafft, zu den größten Uebeln leiten.
„Wär ich doch entfernt geblieben, unbewundert und allein!
„Oder könnt in öden Inseln, oder dort im Norden seyn,
„Wo kein Fahrweg bey der Last goldner Kutschen niedersinket,
„Keine Seele Lomber spielt, und kein Mensch je Caffe trinket.
„Da, da bliebe meine Schönheit allen Sterblichen versteckt,

1. Dieß ist eine Anspielung auf den Schwur des Achilles im Homer, wo Achilles bey seinem Zepter dem Agamemnon schwöret, es werde einmal der Tag kommen, da die Griechen eines Achilles sehr nöthig haben, und Agamemnon ihnen nicht allein würde helfen können. Siehe *Iliad.* I.

Like roses, that in desarts bloom and die.
What mov'd my mind with youthful Lords to roam?
O had I stay'd, and said my pray'rs at home!
'Twas this, the morning omens seem'd to tell,
Thrice from my trembling hand the patch-box fell;
The tott'ring China shook without a wind,
Nay *Poll* sate mute, and *Shock* was most unkind!
A *Sylph* too warn'd me of the threats of fate,
In mystic visions, now believ'd too late!
See the poor remnants of these slighted hairs!
My hands shall rend what ev'n thy rapine spares:
These, in two sable ringlets taught to break,
Once gave new beauties to the snowy neck;
The sister-lock now sits uncouth, alone,
And in its fellow's fate foresees its own;
Uncurl'd it hangs, the fatal sheers demands,
And tempts once more, thy sacrilegious hands.
Oh hadst thou, cruel! been content to seize
Hairs less in sight, or any hairs but these!

Canto V.

She said: the pitying audience melt in tears.
But Fate and *Jove* had stopp'd the Baron's ears.
In vain *Thalestris* with reproach assails,
For who can move when fair *Belinda* fails?
Not half so fix'd the *Trojan* could remain,
While *Anna* begg'd and *Dido* rage'd in vain.
Then grave *Clarissa* graceful wav'd her fan;
Silence ensu'd, and thus the nymph began.
Say why are Beauties prais'd and honour'd most,[1]
The wise man's passion, and the vain man's toast?
Why deck'd with all that land and sea afford,
Why Angels call'd, and Angel-like ador'd?
Why round our coaches croud the white-glov'd Beaus,
Why bows the side-box from its inmost rows?
How vain are all these glories, all our pains,

1. VER. 9, &c. Parody of the Speech of *Sarpedon* to *Glaucus* in *Homer*.

„Wie die Ros' in Wüsten blühet, welket, und den Grund bedeckt.
„Warum nahm ich immermehr junge Stutzer zum spazieren?
„Warum blieb ich nicht daheim, mein Gebethbuch zu studieren?
„Hierauf giengen alle Zeichen, die ich heute nicht verstund:
„Dreymal fiel das Pflasterbüchschen aus den Händen auf den Grund;
„Das erregte Porcelan taumelte von selbst im Zimmer;
„War mein Papagey nicht stumm? und mein Hündchen biß nur immer?
„Selbst ein *Sylphe* hat die Drohung des Geschickes mir gewährt,
„Und was ich zuspät jetzt glaube, durch Gesichter heut erklärt.
„Seht den schlechten Ueberrest von den hochbeschimpften Haaren!
„Meine Faust zerrütte selbst, was der Raub noch konnte sparen.
„Diese Locke war gewöhnet, daß sie in zween Ringeln hieng,
„Als wodurch der weiße Nacken doppelt neuen Glanz empfieng.
„Nunmehr sitzt die andre noch ganz allein, und ganz verstellet;
„Weil aus ihrer Schwester Fall ihr Verhängniß auch erhellet.
„Trauervoll fällt sie zusammen, seufzet gleichfalls nach dem Stahl,
„Und versuchet deinen Frevel, Räuber! noch zum andernmal.
„Grausamer! erschrickst du nicht, daß du, wider dein Gewissen,
„Dieses Kleinod meinem Haupt mit verruchter Faust entrissen?

Ende des vierten Buchs.

Das fünfte Buch.

Dieses sagt sie; jedem wird Zähr und Mitleid abgelocket:
Aber das Geschick und *Zevs* hatten den *Baron* verstocket.
Drohn und Schmähen sind vergebens, das *Thalestris* angeführt:
Denn wer kann die Kunst zu rühren, wenn *Belindens* Reiz nicht rührt?
Des *Trojaners*[1] Härtigkeit hatte nichts, das dieß erreichte.
Den der *Dido* wilde Wuth, *Annens* Flehen nicht erweichte.
Darauf regte sich *Clarissa*; alles schwieg und gab wohl Acht,
Als sie bey geschwungnem Fächer diese Lehren vorgebracht:
„Warum wird die Schönheit doch so erhoben und verehret?
„Aller Weisen Leidenschaft, die die Eiteln auch bethöret.
„Warum deckt man sie mit Schätzen, die so Land als See nur kennt?
„Warum wird sie gleich den Engeln angebethet und genennt?
„Warum dringt der Stutzer Heer weiß behandschucht um die Wagen?
„Warum werden wir gegrüßt, wenn wir uns ins Schauspiel tragen?
„O wie eitel ist dieß Pralen und die Arbeit angewandt;

1. Aeneas, welcher ungeachtet der verliebten Dido, Königinn von Carthago, und des Flehens ihrer Schwester Anna, mit seinen Schiffen fortfuhr. Siehe Virgils 4 Buch.

Unless good sense preserve what beauty gains:
That men may say, when we the front-box grace,
Behold the first in virtue, as in face!
Oh! if to dance all night, and dress all day,
Charm'd the small-pox, or chas'd old-age away;
Who would not scorn what houswife's cares produce,
Or who would learn one earthly thing of use?
To patch, nay ogle, might become a Saint,
Nor could it sure be such a sin to paint.
But since, alas! frail beauty must decay,
Curl'd or uncurl'd, since Locks will turn to grey;
Since painted, or not painted, all shall fade,
And she who scorns a man, must die a maid;
What then remains but well our pow'r to use,
And keep good-humour still whate'er we lose?
And trust me, dear! good-humour can prevail,
When airs, and flights, and screams, and scolding fail.
Beauties in vain their pretty eyes may roll;
Charms strike the sight, but merit wins the soul.
So spoke the Dame, but no applause ensu'd;[1]
Belinda frown'd, *Thalestris* call'd her Prude.
To arms, to arms! the fierce Virago cries,
And swift as lightning to the combat flies.
All side in parties, and begin th'attack;
Fans clap, silks russle, and tough whalebones crack;
Heroes and Heroines shouts confus'dly rise,
And base, and treble voices strike the skies.
No common weapons in their hands are found,
Like Gods they fight, nor dread a mortal wound.
So when bold *Homer* makes the Gods engage,[2]
And heav'nly breasts with human passions rage;
'Gainst *Pallas*, *Mars*; *Latona*, *Hermes* arms;
And all *Olympus* rings with loud alarms:
Jove's thunder roars, heav'n trembles all around;
Blue *Neptune* storms, the bellowing deeps resound;
Earth shakes her nodding tow'rs, the ground gives way,
And the pale ghosts start at the flash of day!

1. It is a verse frequently repeated in *Homer* after any speech,
So spoke — and all the Heroes applauded.
2. Homer, *Il.* 20.

„Wo nicht die Vernunft behauptet, was der Schönheit Fessel band!
„Wo die Welt nicht sagen kann, wenn wie uns im Schauplatz zeigen,
„Schaut! der ist die Tugend so, wie der Reiz, vor allen, eigen!
„Ach! daß doch kein nächtlich Tanzen, und das Putzen Tag für Tag,
„Uns der Blattern Schimpf verjagen, und das Alter bannen mag!
„O wer würde dann sich nicht von der Wirthschaftskunst entfernen!
„O wer wollte dann ein Ding, welches nützlich wär, erlernen?
„Ja, wenn dieses möglich wäre, käm es auch der Frommen ein,
„Sich bepflastern, schminken, äugeln, könnte keine Sünde seyn.
„Aber ach! der Reiz verschwindt bey den allerschönsten Frauen,
„Und, gekräuselt oder nicht! muß doch jede Locke grauen.
„Da auch ein geschminktes Antlitz gleich der andern Haut verdirbt,
„Und die, der kein Mann gefallen, endlich noch als Jungfer stirbt:
„O so bleibt uns nur der Rath, keine Macht zu hoch zu treiben,
„Und, wenn alles sonst vergeht, dennoch gutes Muths zu bleiben.
„Und gewiß, ein froh Gemüthe, das erhält uns, liebstes Kind!
„Wenn das Seufzen, das Erblassen, Schreyn und Keifen fruchtlos sind.
„Hier kann der verliebtste Blick einer Buhlerinn nicht taugen:
„Tugend hält die Seelen fest; Schönheit fesselt nur die Augen.
Also sprach das spröde Fräulein; niemand aber fiel ihr bey.
Selbst *Belinde* sah sehr sauer: der *Thalestris* rege Treu
Schalt sie gar ein sprödes Mensch. Diese schrie: Auf! auf zum Fechten,
Und drang sich zuerst hervor, mit der Feindinn selbst zu rechten.
Alles stellet sich in Ordnung; und nun hört man in der Schlacht
Fächer klappen, Stoffe rauschen; mancher Rock von Fischbein kracht.
Held und Heldinn laufen hier mit dem größesten Getümmel,
Baß, Discant und Mittelstimm dringen durch die Luft zum Himmel.
Doch weil nichts von ihren Waffen von gemeinem Zeuge war,
Fechten sie so, wie die Götter: keine Wunde bringt Gefahr.
So verwegen hat *Homer*[1] seine Götter aufgeführet,
Die in ihrer Himmelsbrust unsrer Rachgier Wuth gespüret.
Pallas kämpfte mit dem *Kriegsgott*; mit *Latonen Majens* Sohn;
Das *olympische* Gebirge füllt ein kriegerischer Ton.
Bald brüllt *Jovens* Donnerknall, und des Himmels Sphären beben;
Auch der blaue *Fischgott* stürmt, dem die Tiefen Antwort geben:
Selbst der feste Boden spaltet, Grund und Erde weichen aus.
Und des Abgrunds scheuen Geistern bringt das Licht Gefahr und Graus.

1. Siehe das 2 Buch der Illias.

Triumphant *Umbriel* on a sconce's height[1]
Clap'd his glad wings, and sate to view the fight:
Prop'd on their bodkin spears, the Sprites survey
The growing combat, or assist the fray.
While thro' the press enrag'd *Thalestris* flies,
And scatters deaths around from both her eyes,
A Beau and Witling perish'd in the throng,
One dy'd in metaphor, and one in song.
"O cruel nymph! a living death I bear,
Cry'd *Dapperwit*, and sunk beside his chair.
A mournful glance Sir *Fopling* upwards cast,
Those eyes are made so killing — was his last.[2]
Thus on *Mæander's* flow'ry margin lies[3]
Th' expiring *Swan*, and as he sings he dies.
When bold Sir *Plume* had drawn *Clarissa* down,
Chloe stepp'd in, and kill'd him with a frown;
She smil'd to see the doughty hero slain,
But, at her smile, the Beau reviv'd again.
Now *Jove* suspends his golden scales in air,[4]
Weighs the Men's wits against the Lady's hair;
The doubtful beam long nods from side to side;
At length the wits mount up, the hairs subside.
See fierce *Belinda* on the Baron flies,
With more than usual lightning in her eyes:
Nor fear'd the Chief th'unequal fight to try,
Who sought no more than on his foe to die.
But this bold Lord with manly strength endu'd,
She with one finger and a thumb subdu'd:
Just where the breath of life his nostrils drew,
A charge of Snuff the wily virgin threw;
The *Gnomes* direct, to ev'ry atome just,
The pungent grains of titillating dust.
Sudden, with starting tears each eye o'erflows,
And the high dome re-echoes to his nose.

1. *Minerva* in like manner, during the Battle of *Ulysses* with the Suitors in *Odyss.* perches on a beam of the roof to behold it.
2. *The Words of a Song in the Opera of* Camilla.
3. Ov. Ep. *Sic ubi fata vocant, udis abjectus in herbis,*
Ad vada Mæandri concinit albus olor.
4. *Vid.* Homer *Il.* 8 & Virg. *Æn.* 12.

Umbriel saß hocherfreut, an der Wand, auf einem Spiegel,
Sah den Streit von weitem zu, und schlug im Triumph die Flügel:
Da die Schaar der andern Geister auf den Zitternadeln sitzt,
Und des Lärmens Wachsthum schauet, oder das Gefecht erhitzt.
Endlich dringt *Thalestris* sich durch dieß wutherfüllte Streiten,
Ihrer schönen Augen Paar droht den Tod auf allen Seiten.
Schaut den *Stutzer* und den *Witzling*, die sie um das Leben bringt!
Einer stirbt in Metaphoren, und der andre, weil er singt.
Schnellwitz sprach: „O hartes Kind! um dich muß ich leben sterben!
Und gleich sah man ihn erblaßt neben seinem Stuhl verderben.
Und Herr *Laffe* kehrt die Augen ganz erstarret in die Höh,
Singend: „Ihr geliebten Augen, bringt zwar lauter Tod und Weh—[1]
Dieses war sein letztes Wort; wie am Ufer von *Mäandern*[2],
Mancher abgelebte Schwan singend aus der Welt muß wandern.
Da Herr *Feder* die *Clarissa* gänzlich umzuwerfen droht,
Naht sich *Chloe*, und ihr Anblick macht ihn augenblicklich todt.
Herzlich lacht sie, daß ihr Blick solche Helden weis zu morden;
Doch da dieß der Stutzer sah, ist er wieder lebend worden.
Zevs ergreift die goldne Wage[3] von dem hohen Göttersitz,
Legt darauf der Schönen Locken, und der jungen Stutzer Witz.
Lange wankt das Schalenpaar, eh der strenge Balken winket;
Endlich steigt der Stutzer Witz, und die schöne Locke sinket.
Hierauf eilet auch *Belinde* voller Eifer zum *Baron*,
Mehr als ein gewöhnlich Feuer herrscht in ihren Blicken schon.
Ob der Kampf schon ungleich war, dennoch scheut er kein Verderben,
Er, der sich nichts mehr gewünscht, als durch diesen Feind zu sterben.
Dieser Held voll Muth und Feuer, der vor allen tapfer hieß,
Fiel sogleich, da ihn *Belinde* nur mit einem Finger stieß:
Und indem er, sonder Kraft, will den schwachen Othem blasen,
Schüttet sie ihm Schnupftaback in die Löcher seiner Nasen.
Umbriel vertheilet die Stäubchen, die dieß scharfe Pulver giebt,
So geschickt, daß es dem *Freyherrn* in das ganze Hirn verstiebt.
Man erblickt den Zährenstrom aus den rothen Augen dringen,
Und das Kirchdach muß den Laut seiner Nase wiederbringen.

1. Dieß ist eine Arie aus einer englischen Oper, *Camilla* genannt.
2. Dieses ist ein Fluß in klein Asien, der von den Griechen Μαίανδρος genennet worden, anjetzt aber *Madre* oder *Mindre*, wie auch *Boiuk Mindre*, das ist, der große Meander genennet wird. Er entspringt auf dem Berge *Aulocrene* aus einem See, und fließt mit wunderbaren Krümmen durch *Apamea*, *Eumenetica*, *Carien* und *Ionien*, bis er sich endlich in das *Mare Myrtourn* ergießt. Homer soll an diesem Fluße gebohren seyn, daher er auch oftmals *Maeonides* genennet wird.
3. Auf diese Weise läßt *Homer* im 8 Buche des *Ilias* den *Jupiter* auf dem Berge *Ida*, das Schicksal der Griechen und Trojaner abwägen.

Now meet thy fate, incens'd *Belinda* cry'd,
And drew a deadly bodkin from her side.
(The same, his ancient personage to deck,[1]
Her great great grandsire wore about his neck,
In three seal-rings; which after, melted down,
Form'd a vast buckle for his widow's gown:
Her infant grandame's whilstle next it grew,

1. *In imitation of the progress of* Agamemnon's *sceptre in* Homer, *Il.* 2.

„Unterwirf dich nun dem Schicksal! ruft *Belinde* ganz ergrimmt,
Da sie aus den Seitenhaaren eine Mördernadel[1] nimmt.
Diese pflegt ihr Ahnherr sonst, seinen alten Leib zu zieren,
In drey Siegelringen stets um den dürren Hals[2] zu führen;
Die man nachmals eingeschmolzen, und an seiner Wittwe Tracht
Eine ungeheure Schnalle zu dem Leibgurt draus gemacht.
Hierauf ists ein Kinderspiel ihrer *Großmama* gewesen,

1. Herr Pope bezieht sich hier wiederum auf den Homer, welcher im 2 B. der *Ilias* eine, wiewohl sehr kurze Beschreibung von *Agamemnons* Zepter macht, daß er ihn nämlich von seinen Vorfahren überkommen, und daß selbiger in dessen Geschlechte unsterblich sey. Ich gestehe, daß ich nicht weis, was Pope mit dieser und den bisherigen Anführungen eigentlich haben wollen. Will er seine Ausdrücke, Beschreibungen und Figuren mit Homers Ansehen schützen? Aber steht es denn nicht einem jeden Dichter frey, zu schreiben wie er will, so lange er bey den allgemeinen Regeln bleibt? Oder will er zeigen, daß er den Homer gelesen? Daran wird man ja bey einem Manne nicht zweifeln, der ihn gar übersetzt hat. Oder will er endlich den guten Homer lächerlich machen? Ist dieß; so gelingt ihm sein Endzweck sehr schlecht. Denn darum, daß ein gewisser Schwur, oder eine Beschreibung, oder eine Handlung, in einem lustigen Gedichte lächerlich sind; darum sind sie es noch nicht in einem ernsthaften. Es ist ja eben ein großer Kunstgriff der poßierlichen Schreibart, daß sie hohe Ausdrücke zu niedern Sachen brauche, und große feyerliche Anstalten zu geringen Begebenheiten dichte. Ich weis zwar, daß der Graf Shaftsbury die Regel giebt, man soll, als eine Probe, ob ein Ausdruck gut sey, das annehmen, wenn er sich nicht lächerlich machen läßt. Allein wie ist das möglich, wofern er sich nicht zu allen Sachen und in allen Fällen schicket? Denn sobald man ihn zu einer ungehörigen Sache nehmen wird, so wird er lächerlich. Ich bin auf diese letzte Anmerkung, den Homer betreffend, darum gekommen, weil sich auch unter unsern Deutschen unlängst einige auf scherzhafte Heldengedichte beflissen, und einige von ihnen geglaubt haben: sie schrieben schon aufgeweckt und scharfsinnig, wenn sie nur hier und da den Homer durch eine ungehörige Anwendung seiner Ausdrücke, oder Beschreibungen, lächerlich machten. Vielleicht hat Pope sie hierzu verführt; vielleicht aber haben sie ihn auch nicht recht verstanden. Denn vor solchen Mitteln lächerlich zu werden, ist das heiligste und erhabenste, ja die ernsthafteste Beschreibung von der Welt nicht gesichert: wie solches alle Parodien der Franzosen, auf ihre besten Trauerspiele bezeugen können.
2. Ich hatte anfangs gesetzt: *an der dürren Hand zu führen*; weil ich mir gar keinen Begriff von der englischen Zeile

   Her great great Grandsire wore about his neck
   In three Seal-rings.

   machen konnte. Allein ich habe von ungefähr im Zinkgräf eine Stelle gefunden, die mich lehret, daß dieses eine alte Mode gewesen. Weil diese Stelle nicht lang ist, so will ich sie ganz hersetzen: ‘Als der Obriste, Peter Beuterich von Newenfelß, zu Straßburg, neben etlichen von Adel zu einer Gasterey war, und einen goldenen Pitschierring, auf dem sein Wapen mit einem offnen Helm, geschnitten, an einer seidenen Schnur, (wie damals gebräuchlich) am Halse hangen hatte, und einer vom Adel nach demselben griffe, und es besehen wollte, sagte Beutrich zu ihm: Gemach darmit, es ist noch gar frisch, daß ihrs nicht zerbrechet. Dadurch er sich als ein Neugeadelter, selbst vexierte, doch sagte er dabey: Er wolle lieber der erste, als der letzte seines Geschlechtes seyn.’ Siehe deutscher Nation klugausgesprochene Weisheit, im I Theile die 146 Seite, der Amsterdamer Ausgabe von 1654.

The bells she jingled, and the whistle blew;
Then in a bodkin grac'd her mother's hairs,
Which long she wore, and now *Belinda* wears.)
Boast not my fall (he cry'd) insulting foe!
Thou by some other shalt be laid as low.
Nor think, to die dejects my lofty mind:
All that I dread is leaving you behind!
Rather than so, ah let me still survive,
And burn in *Cupid's* flames, — but burn alive.
Restore the Lock! she cries; and all around
Restore the Lock! the vaulted roofs rebound.
Not fierce *Othello* in so loud a strain
Roar'd for the handkerchief that caus'd his pain.
But see how oft ambitious aims are cross'd,
And chiefs contend 'till all the prize is lost!
The Lock, obtain'd with guilt, and kept with pain,
In ev'ry place is sought, but sought in vain:
With such a prize no mortal must be blest,
So heav'n decrees! with heav'n who can contest?
Some thought it mounted to the Lunar sphere,
Since all things lost on earth are treasur'd there.[1]
There Hero's wits are kept in pond'rous vases,
And Beau's in snuff boxes and tweezer-cases.
There broken vows, and death-bed alms are found,
And lovers hearts with ends of ribband bound,
The courtier's promises, and sick man's pray'rs,
The smiles of harlots, and the tears of heirs,
Cages for gnats, and chains to yoak a flea,
Dry'd butterflies, and tomes of casuistry.
But trust the Muse — she saw it upward rise,
Tho' mark'd by none but quick, poetic eyes:
(So *Rome's* great founder to the heav'ns withdrew,
To *Proculus* alone confess'd in view)
A sudden Star, it shot thro' liquid air,
And drew behind a radiant trail of hair.
Not *Berenice's* Locks first rose so bright,

1. *Vid.* Ariosto, Canto 34.

Die es als ein Pfeifchen blies, und zum Zeitvertreib erlesen.
Dieses ward zur Zitternadel, die schon in der Mutter Haar
Lange Zeit der Schmuck gewesen, der sie bey *Belinden* war.
„Sey nicht stolz auf deinen Sieg, schönes Kind! es wird geschehen,
Rief der *Ritter*, „daß auch du dich einst wirst erniedrigt sehen.
„Zwar der Tod ist meinem Herzen kein so schrecklicher Verdruß;
„Was mich kränkt, ist dieß, *Belinde*, daß ich dich verlieren muß.
„Ehe dieser Fall geschieht, mußt du mir jetzt Gnade gönnen:
„Tödte mich durch Amors Glut; aber laß mich lebend brennen.
„Gieb mir meine Locke wieder! rief sie, und der helle Schall
„Gieb mir meine Locke wieder, klung von jedem Widerhall.
Selbst *Othellens*[1] Raserey hat man nicht so lärmen sehen,
Als man ihm sein Schnupftuch stahl. Aber schaut, wies pflegt zu gehen!
Wie bekriegt sich doch der Hochmuth, wenn der Endzweck ihm mislingt,
Daß man, bis der Preis verschwunden, nach dem edlen Zwecke ringt.
So ward auch dieß schöne Haar, das die Bosheit überwunden,
Und die größte Müh gewann, stark gesucht, und nicht gefunden.
Solch ein Kleinod zu begehren, ist für Sterbliche zu kühn!
Dieses Urtheil sprach der Himmel: und wer kann wohl wider ihn?
Zwar man sagt, sie sey hinauf in den Mondenkreis gestiegen,
Weil, was hier auf Erden schwindt[2], dorten soll verwahret liegen.
Dorten liegt der Witz der Helden in Geschirren schwerer Art,
Und der Stutzer Witz in Dosen und in Büchschen aufbewahrt:
Manches Todbetts Mildigkeit und ein Schwarm gebrochner Eide;
Manch verliebtes Herz umschlingt da ein Band von bunter Seide;
Das Versprechen manches Hofmanns, und der Kranken Reu und Leid,
Nebst dem Lächeln schnöder Metzen; reicher Erben Traurigkeit;
Kefigte fürs Mückenvolk; Flöheketten; trockne Fliegen;
Und der Casuisten Kram sieht man da bey Haufen liegen.
Aber traut nur meiner Muse; diese sah sie aufwärts gehn:
Und das kann, vor allen Menschen, nur ein Dichterauge sehn.
(So hat auch den *Stifter Roms*, vor so vielen hundert Jahren,
Nur ein einzger *Proculus* sehen nach dem Himmel fahren)
Sternengleich sah ich sie schießen an das blaue Himmelsdach,
Ein entbrannter Schweif von Stralen fuhr dem goldnen Körper nach.
Berenicens Locke selbst, die man an dem Himmel malet,

1. Othello ist ein Held in einem englischen Trauerspiele, welcher viele Thränen vergießt, und ein gewaltiges Herzeleid darüber bezeuget, daß man ihm sein Schnuptuch gestohlen, welches er von seiner Geliebten geschenkt bekommen. Dergleichen Possen sind in den englischen Tragödien, die noch zur Zeit sich an keine Regeln binden, nichts neues.
2. Man sehe den Ariost im 34 Gesange; oder Fontenellens Gespräche von mehr als einer Welt, nach der deutschen Uebersetzung. Leipz. Ausg. von 1738, 72 u. f. S.

The heav'ns bespangling with dishevel'd light.
The *Sylphs* behold it kindling as it flies,
And pleas'd pursue its progress thro' the skies.
    This the *Beau-monde* shall from the Mall survey,
And hail with music its propitious ray.
This the blest Lover shall for *Venus* take,
And send up vows from *Rosamonda's* lake.
This *Partridge* soon shall view in cloudless skies,[1]
When next he looks thro' *Galilæo's* eyes;
And hence th' egregious wizard shall foredoom
The fate of *Louis*, and the fall of *Rome*.
    Then cease, bright Nymph! to mourn thy ravish'd hair,
Which adds new glory to the shining sphere!
Not all the tresses that fair head can boast,
Shall draw such envy as the Lock you lost.
For, after all the murders of your eye,
When, after millions slain, yourself shall die;
When those fair suns shall set, as set they must,
And all those tresses shall be laid in dust;
This Lock, the Muse shall consecrate to fame,
And 'midst the stars inscribe *Belinda's* name.

1. VER. 137. *John Partridge* was a ridiculous Star-gazer, who in his Almanacks every year, never fail'd to predict the downfall of the Pope, and the King of *France*, then at war with the *English*.

Hat nicht gleich so wunderschön und so flammenreich gestralet.
Selbst die *Sylphen* sahn mit Freuden, wie er durch die Lüfte flog,
Deren Heer, indem er fortgieng, voller Jauchzen mit ihm zog.
Die galante Stutzerwelt wird es von dem Walle grüßen,
Und desselben Gnadenstral musikalisch ehren müssen.
Der beglückte Buhler denket, Venus strale von der Höh
Und schickt ihr noch manch Gelübde von dem *Rosamunder See*[1].
Auch *Partridge*[2] wird darnach bey entwölktem Himmel gehen,
Wenn er nächstens wieder wird mit crystallnen Augen sehen.
Dieser große Zeichendeuter wird aus dieser Locke Schein
Uns den Untergang des Pabstthums, *Ludwigs* Sterben, prophezeyn.
Schönste Nymphe! laß denn nach, diese Locke zu beklagen,
Die der heitern Himmelsburg so viel Zierde zugetragen.
Keines Hauptes Wunderlocken, die der Schönen Stolz verführt,
Werden so viel Neid erwecken, als die jetzt dein Haupt verliert.
Denn nach so viel Mord und Tod, die dein Augenstral erreget,
Wenn nach Millionen Sieg, du dich selbst ins Grab geleget,
Wenn die beyden schönen Sonnen, wie sie müssen, untergehn,
Wenn man alle deine Locken wird in Staub und Asche sehn:
Dann wird diese Locke, bloß durch die Musen übrig bleiben,
Und man wird ins Sternenheer noch *Belindens* Namen schreiben.

ENDE.

OVID Met. L. XV.

Simul euolat illa
Flammiserumque trahens spatioso lumine crinem
Stella micat.

1. Dieß ist ein See bey Londen, der deswegen schon lächerlich ist, weil sich einige Verliebten darinnen ersäufet haben.
2. Dieses war ein seltsamer Calendermacher in London, der ein großer Sterndeuter seyn wollte, und jährlich viel närrische Prophezeyungen in seine Calender setzte; insonderheit wollte er aus allen Begebenheiten den Verfall des Pabstthums, und den Tod des Königes von Frankreich, Ludwigs des XIV. vorherverkündigen. Er ist aber von dem bekannten *D. Swift* sehr gedemüthiget worden, der eine Verkündigung von dem eigenen bevorstehenden Tode dieses *Partridge* drucken ließ, worüber sie zu lustigen Streitschriften mit einander gekommen sind. Wer von den deutschen Lesern dieselben nachschlagen will, der wird sie bey der Uebersetzung des *Mährchens von der Tonne*, welche hier zu Leipzig im 1729 Jahre herausgekommen ist, auf der 206 und folgenden Seite mit vielem Vergnügen lesen können.

Anhang

Freye Uebersetzung
der
EPITRE CHAGRINE
in den Poësies
de Mad[me] DESHOULIERES
Tom. 1. pag. 32. übersetzt 1736.

Was quält, o Freundinn! dich für ein verkehrter Wahn?
Wo rührt der Ehrgeiz her, der dich so fesseln kann?
Du willst ja gar gelehrt, und zur Poetinn werden!
Ach, Iris! kennst du auch die Menge der Beschwerden,
Die der verwünschte Ruf der Dichtkunst nach sich zieht?
So hoch man ihren Werth in alten Zeiten sieht,
So niedrig steht er jetzt. Ihr Lorber ist zerrissen!
Das ist das höchste Lob: Nichts schreiben, und nichts wissen!

Wann der verhaßte Ruf in einer Stadt erklingt,
Daß wieder eine Frau nach Art der Dichter singt:
So wird sie ganz gewiß, zum Lohne solcher Gaben,
Nicht die geringste Gunst des Glücks zu hoffen haben.
Ein jeder tadelt sie, man sagt ihr Uebels nach:
Warum? sie hat Verstand! das ist genug zur Schmach.
Und wenn gleich Geist und Witz sie zur Theano machen;
So wird man sie gewiß, zum wenigsten, verlachen.

Zwar hat das Schicksal dich mit Gütern wohl versehn,
Du willst durch Verse nicht dein Brod erbetteln gehn:
Wer gäbe dir auch was in diesen kargen Tagen?
Da sich die Musen selbst mit Frost und Blöße plagen.

Du reimest nur zur Lust; und machst dir keinen Staat
Auf großer Herren Gunst. Das ist nun in der That,
Ein Unglück weniger. Doch, lies nur diese Zeilen,
Die werden, Iris, dir den Unterricht ertheilen,
Was dir noch sonsten droht. Bedenk es in der Zeit,
Wie mancher schwere Schlag den Musenfreunden dräut.
Hier hast du meinen Rath, das Zeugniß meiner Treue;
Damit dein schneller Schluß dich nicht zu spät gereue.

Bedenke nur zuerst, ob dirs Vergnügen bringt,
Wann ein Pedantenschwarm zu dir ins Zimmer dringt.
Mich dünkt, es wimmelt schon von närrischen Poeten,
Die spielen nach der Reih, auf ungeübten Flöten,
Dir ihre Lieder vor; die nur in letzter Nacht
Ihr Unsinn ausgeheckt, ein Rausch ans Licht gebracht.
Die wollen nun von dir, mit ehrsuchtsvollen Sinnen,
Ein abgedrungnes Lob, für ihre Müh gewinnen.

Dort kömmt ein junger Herr mit freyem Schritt herein,
Der kaum recht lesen kann. Der schwert nun Stein und Bein:
Dein neues Werk gebiehrt dir minder Ruhm als Schande!
Ertrag es! denn es ist ein Geck von hohem Stande.

Solch ein verkehrter Geist hat jetzt die Welt bethört!
Es wird kein Weiser mehr mit Lehrbegier gehört.
Man kauft kein neues Buch, aus Lust zu guten Sachen:
Man liest die Bücher nur den Schreiber auszulachen.
Das ist für lange Müh der schwer erworbne Lohn!
Man biethet allem Witz in unsern Schriften Hohn;
Und jeder dumme Kopf, den nur die Ahnen adeln,
Glaubt fest, er hab ein Recht, das beste Buch zu tadeln.

Du denkst, ich stelle mir nur Hirngespinste vor;
Die Eigenliebe zischt dir heimlich in das Ohr:
Ich thäte dir zu viel, und wollte dich nur plagen,
Es würde dir die Welt den Beyfall nie versagen.
Ganz gut! gesetzt, du kömmst in ein bekanntes Haus:
Kaum rufet der Lackey nur deinen Namen aus:
So hört man alsobald den Schall von allen Seiten:
Das ist ein kluges Weib, die Sappho unsrer Zeiten!

Drauf fängt man ein Gespräch von neuen Schriften an:
Man denkt, du weist sonst nichts: Dann fragt dich jedermann:
Ob Phyllis wohl ihr Buch aus eignem Kopf geschrieben?
Und ob sie nicht vielleicht ein fremder Geist getrieben?
Ob denn ihr neues Werk auch deinen Ruhm erhält?
Ein jeder spricht, daß ihm dein Dichten sehr gefällt:
Zumal dein letzter Vers wird dir den Preis erjagen.
Drum zwingt man dich, davon drey Strophen herzusagen.

Ist nun dein Vortrag nicht ganz voller Schwulst und Dunst;
So sagt man sich ins Ohr: Ist das die große Kunst?
Klingt denn auch dieß gelehrt? Das kann ich doch nicht sehen:
Denn alles was sie sagt, das kann man ja verstehen!

Du sprichst: Ach sorge nicht, daß wird mir nicht geschehn;
Dem Uebel will ich schon mit leichter Müh entgehn.
Ich darf die große Zahl der Thoren nur vermeiden;
So darf ich ihren Trotz und dummen Spott nicht leiden.

Ganz wohl! Doch dir entfällt der schmerzliche Verdruß,
Den Witz, Verstand und Kunst bey Höfen dulden muß.
Du willst dich von der Pracht des Hofes nicht entfernen:
Gut, Iris! bleibe nur! du wirsts mit Schaden lernen,
Wie gut ich es gemeynt; und daß es richtig sey,
Was dir mein Kiel hier schreibt. Ich rede nicht zu frey:
Die Hofluft ist gewiß ein tödlich Gift zu nennen,
Für alle die Geschmack, Vernunft, und Wissen kennen.

O! sperre zeitig dich in einen Winkel ein,
Da wird dein eigner Witz dein bester Umgang seyn.
Denn wann sich in der Stadt der Ruf nur ausgebreitet;
Daß dich ein innrer Trieb zum Musenhügel leitet:
So haßt dich alle Welt! so flieht dich Weib und Mann!
Warum denn? weil man sich auf nichts besinnen kann:
Und wollte man sich gleich zehn Jahr den Kopf zerbrechen,
Was man mit dir beginnt? was man mit dir wird sprechen?

Die Ursach dieser Furcht bethört die ganze Stadt.
Man denkt: ein Frauenbild, das Lust zu Künsten hat,
Und sich den Musen weiht, verhöhnt die Weibersachen,
Und kann sonst weiter nichts, als lauter Verse machen.

Der Dichtkunst hohen Stoff, den uns die Fabel lehrt,
Und was den seltnen Ruhm der Alterthümer mehrt,
Muß man nach ihrem Sinn, als Kleinigkeiten meiden:
Wer mehr versteht als sie, den können sie nicht leiden.

Bringt man für andre nun ein neues Stück herein;
So dringt ein jeder zu, und will dein Richter seyn.
Sie setzen sich dahin wie Midas sonst gesessen,
Als er des Phöbus Kunst nach seinem Kopf gemessen.
Doch, niemand irre sich: es ist ein bloßer Schein.
Oft dringt das zehnte Wort nicht in ihr Ohr hinein;
Noch öftrer haben sie gar nichts davon verstanden:
Doch wird das Blatt gelobt! doch macht man es zu Schanden!
Wenn nur ein schwülstig Wort in einer Zeile steht:
So wird das ganze Werk gepriesen und erhöht.
Ein Wort scheint hart zu seyn; und wer kann das vermeiden?
Genug! das Urtheil fällt: das Stück ist nicht zu leiden!

Mops, dessen kaltes Blut ein starker Wein erhitzt,
Der bey den Karten mehr, als bey den Büchern sitzt,
Will auf der Richterbank auch einen Platz erreichen:
Man hört ihn den Homer mit dem Horaz vergleichen.
Wer kennt den Unterschied von diesen Dichtern nicht?
Doch Mops, dem Witz und Geist, und Wissenschaft gebricht,
Vermischet ihre Kunst, verwechselt ihre Schriften,
Und sucht durch diesen Schluß sich noch ein Lob zu stiften:
Daß beyden vieles fehlt, daß es ein Spielwerk heißt,
Was man an beyden doch als unvergleichlich preist.
So sucht sich unser Mops in Sprachen und in Sachen,
Davon er nichts versteht, recht breit und groß zu machen.

Zwar weis ich, daß man noch ein Paar von Großen findt,
Die noch ein Ueberrest des alten Hofes sind.
Die schützen freylich wohl die halberstorbnen Künste,
Und diesen bleibt das Lob der Nachwelt zum Gewinnste.
Allein, wie lang hinaus erstreckt ihr Leben sich?
Hier sträubet sich das Haar! die Furcht erschüttert mich!
Ihr silberweißes Haupt naht sich bereits den Sternen,
Mit diesen wird sich auch Geschmack und Geist entfernen!

Dann zieht die Unvernunft zu unsern Thoren ein!
Dann wird das ganze Land ein Raub der Dummheit seyn!
Dann wird den Musen selbst vor unsern Grenzen grauen!
Dann kriegt die Barbarey uns wieder in die Klauen!

Dann glaub ich, ganz gewiß, wofern mein Geist nicht irrt,
Daß dich dein eigner Witz noch schamroth machen wird!
Da wirst du ganz allein in deinem Winkel singen,
Da wird kein Kenner sich zu deinen Zimmern dringen.
Ja, zweifle nur nicht mehr! wir sehn ja mit Verdruß,
Wie manches Beyspiel uns den Satz erweisen muß:
Was macht man doch mit Witz? was strebt man nach Verstande?
Was nützen sie der Stadt? was helfen sie dem Lande?

Ach, liebste Freundinn! gieb dem treuen Rath Gehör!
Ersticke deinen Trieb, und lerne nur nichts mehr!
Wenn gleich der Weisheit Ruhm bis an die Wolken dringet;
So glaube, daß er auch mehr Gram, als Freude bringet.
Jetzt kenn ich erst die Frucht die aus dem Wissen keimt;
Hätt ich es ehr gewußt; ich hätte nie gereimt!
Ich hätte nie den Blick auf Pindus ferne Höhen,
Und nie den Fuß gelenkt, den Musen nachzugehen.
Doch, wie kein Sterblicher sein eigner Meister bleibt;

Er folgt dem Triebe nach, der ihn am stärksten treibt:
So hat auch mich mein Stern zum Wissen angeführet,
Eh ich den Schaden sah, den dieser Fleiß gebiehret.
Du, Iris, warst bisher von solchem Triebe frey:
Drum folge meinem Rath, und bleibe doch dabey.
Das Schicksal hat dir Geld und Anmuth gnug gegeben;
Mit diesen läßt es sich vorjetzt am besten leben.
Das aber wirkt gewiß die allergrößte Pein:
In einer dummen Welt, gelehrt und klug zu seyn!

**Uebersetzung
einer andern
EPITRE CHAGRINE
aus den Gedichten
der Frau des HOULIERES.**

Wie? welch ein finstrer Gram ficht auch schon wieder an?
Die Frage hat mir heut ein junger Herr gethan,
Der seiner Schönheit nach, Cupiden selbst nicht weichet,
Dem er an List, Betrug und Falschheit völlig gleichet.
Ihr schweigt? Was fehlt euch denn? So fuhr er weiter fort,
Und fluchte gar dazu. So sprecht doch nur ein Wort!
Bin ich vielleicht nicht werth, daß ihr es mir entdecket,
Was für ein stiller Schmerz euch in dem Kopfe stecket?
Ja, ja! ich mag euch wohl zu schlecht und niedrig seyn!
Hier schloß er sein Geschwätz; und lachte hönisch drein.
Drauf ward mein Wunsch erfüllt: er gieng davon, mit Fluchen,
Mehr Leute seiner Art, mehr Gecken aufzusuchen.

Was hätt ich ihm auch wohl auf alles dieß gesagt?
Ich, welche damals gleich ein wahrer Schmerz geplagt,
Weil ich des Hofes Art mir zu Gemüth gezogen,
Und dieser neuen Zeit gewohnten Lauf erwogen.
Wie hätt er sich erboßt, wenn meine Redlichkeit,
Ihm ohne Heucheley, die Schande seiner Zeit
Recht lebhaft abgemalt? und wenn ich ihm beschrieben
Die Laster, die er selbst gewohnt ist auszuüben?
Hier hätte Zorn und Wuth der Wahrheit nicht geschont,
Und meine Redlichkeit mit Raserey belohnt.
Doch, suchte mich auch gleich sein Eifer zu ertödten;
So würd er nicht einmal vor seiner Schmach erröthen.

Die Kühnheit kenn ich schon, die solche Seelen nährt,

Sie denken, was sie thun, sey alles lobenswerth;
Sie fühlen weder Scham noch Ehrgeiz in dem Herzen,
Man hört sie ungescheut mit eignen Lastern scherzen.
Es braucht kein fremdes Blatt, daraus ihr Thun erhellt,
Sie selbst erzählen es, ohn alle Scheu, der Welt:
Indem sie frechheitsvoll die ärgsten Laster sagen,
Dabey auch Knechte wohl die Augen niederschlagen.
Die Richtschnur der Vernunft, Gesetz, Philosophie,
Die sind, so wie es scheint, für andre, nicht für sie.
Der ärgsten Laster Wust, der Abschaum frecher Zeiten,
Das nennt man Artigkeit, das sind nur Kleinigkeiten.

Sie widmen ihre Gunst den Leuten schlechter Art;
Dem Pöbel bleibt ihr Herz und Umgang vorgespart:
Drum fällt ihr Ansehn auch. Wenn haben solche Sitten,
Bey Seelen edler Art sich Ehr und Ruhm erstritten?
In Wahrheit, nimmermehr! Des Adels Ansehn fällt,
Wenn nicht die Lebensart der Ahnen Glanz erhält.
Dann kömmt der Stand, den sie durch die Geburt besessen,
Auch andern aus dem Sinn: weil sie ihn selbst vergessen.

Kömmt ihnen ja die Lust uns zu besuchen, ein;
So darf der strengste Mann nicht eifersüchtig seyn:
Sie kommen ganz gewiß nicht unsrer Anmuth wegen,
Sie glauben gar, es sey uns keine beyzulegen.
Sie plappern nur von sich und mancher dummen That:
Wie hoch sie jüngst gespielt, und wer gewonnen hat.
Es ist ein neuer Wein aus Welschland angekommen;
Und dessen Probe wird den Abend vorgenommen.
Trax zeigt den Liebesbrief, den ihm Climene gab,
Und schwört, daß sie ihn liebt; nur er schlägt alles ab.
Die andern wackeln sich im pfeifen auf den Stühlen;
Wofern sie nicht zur Lust mit ihren Hunden spielen.
Ein Theil spaziert indeß im Zimmer hin und her,
Und thut als wenn er recht bey sich zu Hause wär.
Wenn dieß Bezeigen uns nun lange gnug gequälet;
So wird von ihnen noch die Abendlust erwählet.
Man nennt den besten Wirth, bestimmet Zeit und Ort,
Und geht mit Ungestüm, oft sonder Abschied, fort.

Ist einer in der Zahl, den noch die Menschheit rühret,
Der einen innern Trieb zur Artigkeit verspüret;
Der zwar oft zärtlich scheint, jedoch auch Ehrfurcht nährt,

Verdienst und Anmuth stärkt, ja, welcher ewig währt:
So wird der ganze Schwarm sich alsobald befleißen,
Ihn weiblich, dumm, und blind und ungeschickt zu heißen.
Wenn er der edlen Glut nicht gleich den Rücken kehrt;
So bleibt kein Schimpf zurück, der ihm nicht wiederfährt:
Und die Verachtung wird so lange fortgetrieben,
Bis er sich selber schämt nach edler Art zu lieben.

Die Höflichkeit, die man den Schönen schuldig ist,
Das ist der erste Satz, den dieses Volk vergißt.
Wer an der Hand sie führt; das ist schon ein Verbrechen!
Von einer Schönen Witz, von ihrer Anmuth sprechen:
Das schenkt man nimmermehr! das wird so lang verlacht;
Bis Beyspiel, Müh und Spott, den Tölpel fertig macht.

Wo ist die alte Zeit? Wo sind die schönen Stunden,
Allwo die Tugend auch bey Großen Platz gefunden?
Wo seyd ihr doch anjetzt, ihr Seelen bessrer Art?
Bey euch war Stand und Macht mit Höflichkeit gepaart.
Ihr Prinzen, deren Huld den höchsten Grad erreichet,
Seht unsre Jugend an, wie sie dem Pöbel gleichet!
Wo sind die Zeiten ietzt, als Ludwigs Artigkeit
Den Saamen edler Huld in Frankreich ausgestreut?
Da ward der Barbarey, da ward den groben Sitten
Durch diesen Prinzen bald der Nahrungssaft beschnitten.
Hier widersprach man nicht der Ordnung der Natur;
Der Schönen Vorzugsrecht verletzte keine Spur
Der Ungezogenheit. Wo ist die Zeit geblieben!
Die Unvernunft hat sie zu unsrer Quaal vertrieben!

Ach Stunden! kehret doch nur einmal noch zurück;
Vielleicht würd euer Glanz, vielleicht würd euer Blick
Uns wieder zu dem Grad der alten Zucht erheben,
Und unsrer Jugend noch die Ehrfurcht wiedergeben.
Jetzt, da die Wollust sie den Knechten ähnlich macht,
Was Wunder, daß man auch den Wohlstand nur verlacht?
Daß man die Ehre haßt, die Sitten fast nicht kennet,
Und kaum die Tugend noch bey ihrem Namen nennet.
Die Schönen sind ein Ziel der Unbesonnenheit.
Wer uns nichts grobes thut, der übt schon Höflichkeit.
Kurz, unsre Jugend ist verdorben und verlohren,
Das Schicksal hat sie nur zu unsrer Quaal gebohren.

Jedoch, wen plaget hier mein tadelnder Verdruß?

Man straf uns selber nur, wo jemand leiden muß.
Wir selber haben schuld an diesem wilden Leben,
Indem wir ihnen selbst zur Wildheit Anlaß geben.

Warum verstatten wir der Jugend dieser Zeit
Die tolle Lebensart, die Unbesonnenheit?
Man halte sie so scharf als unsre Mütter thaten,
Da Tugend, Scherz und Witz den steten Wettstreit hatten.
Wie? oder glaubet man, daß ihrer Schönheit Pracht,
Ihr Witz, Verstand und Reiz sie kräftiger gemacht,
Als wir anjetzo sind? Wer wollte dieses denken?
Der Vorwurf würd uns ja nur gar zu heftig kränken.
Und doch hat damals sich der Wohlstand nie beklagt,
Daß ihn die Wildheit so, als wie anjetzt verjagt.
Die Klugheit, Zärtlichkeit und Ehrfurcht, war bey allen
(Doch allezeit vereint) der Anfang zum Gefallen.
Der jungen Fürsten Zahl, und was nur edel war,
Die nahm man dazumal in ihren Zimmern wahr.
Und wenn ein kluger Scherz, mit Witz und Lust gewürzet,
Den überbliebnen Rest des Tages froh verkürzet,
Wo niemand seine Lust mit frechen Zoten trieb,
Und wo die reinste Zucht stets unversehret blieb:
So gieng man frölich fort mit eifrigem Verlangen,
Den Morgen wiederum so reizend anzufangen.
Die Liebe dorft hier nie der Tugend widerstehn,
Was man verehrte, war auch, sonder Hoffnung, schön;
Denn reine Triebe, die von wahrer Ehrfurcht stammen,
Kann auch der Himmel selbst zu keiner Zeit verdammen.

Die Zeiten sind vorbey! Wer kennt die unsern nicht?
Man weis, wie vieles hier der Aehnlichkeit gebricht.
Man redet wie man denkt, und denkt wie Mägd und Knechte;
Drum kömmt der Wohlstand auch um alle seine Rechte.
Der Wohlstand, der der Grund von ieder Freundschaft ist.
Und alles strafbar nennt, wobey man ihn vergißt.

Man spricht: Wir müssen uns dem Uebel unterziehen;
Sonst wird man endlich gar die strengen Zimmer fliehen,
Allwo die Tugend stets auf Richterstühlen sitzt.

Gewiß, ein feiner Schluß, der euren Kummer stützt!
Wie groß ist der Verlust? Ich muß ihn doch entdecken:
Der bäurische Tumult? der Umgang junger Gecken?
Ist das die große Noth? Ach! ist das Kreuz nicht schwer!

In euren Häusern sieht man keine Narren mehr!
Kein dummes Lästermaul! Man hört kein lautes Lachen,
Das ohne Grund entsteht. Man spricht von lauter Sachen,
Die ganz vernünftig sind, an welchen jedermann,
Der Salz im Kopfe hat, sich auch ergetzen kann!
Man höret keinen mehr, der sonder Ursach pralet,
Von allen borgen kann, mit lauter Wind bezahlet?
Und kurz, die Schaar, die euch anitzt den Rücken kehrt,
Die hat euch stets verschmäht, und ihr habt sie verehrt!

Allein sie that ganz recht. Die Frechheit eurer Sitten
Hat selbst bey ihr der Lust zur Ehrfurcht widerstritten.
Denn zeigtet ihr an euch der wahren Tugend Schein:
So würden jene bald zur Ehrfurcht fertig seyn.
Jedoch, was klag ich viel? Wen sind ich, der mich höre?
Man läuft den Buhlern nach, zum Nachtheil eigner Ehre!

Ihr schenket ihnen gern Verstand und Artigkeit
Und alle Tugenden; ja auch so gar die Zeit,
Die man zum Wünschen braucht. Ihr gebet, eh sie bitten,
Was man vor diesem erst nach langer Müh erstritten.
Der Liebe letzten Lohn, der nie erkäuflich war,
Den biethet ihr anjetzt auch ungefordert dar.
Die Alten suchen selbst sich Buhler zu erringen,
Und was sie jung versäumt, im Alter einzubringen.

Ach! liebste Daphne! bleib in deiner Einsamkeit,
Die dir mit reiner Lust der Unschuld Umgang weiht,
Und wünsche nimmermehr die Kenntniß unsrer Zeiten,
Und unsrer Jugend selbst. O! schau sie stets von weiten
Mit weisen Augen an! und glaube, daß kein Heer
Von wilden Bestien, kein Tyger, und kein Bär
In einer Wüsteney, so schädlich seyn zu nennen,
Als diese Menschen sind, die wir hier um uns kennen.

COMMENTARY

The English source text is taken from the following edition: *The Works of Alexander Pope, Esq.: With Explanatory Notes and Additions Never Before Printed*, 4 vols (London: Lintot, 1736), I, pp. 142–74. This is the edition which Gottsched had in her library and presumably the one she used for her translation. The only substantial change made to the original text is in the numbering of footnotes: in the source text footnotes include a reference to the relevant line(s) of the poem (e.g. 'VER. 11, 12') or are linked to a line in the poem by a system of symbols (i.e. an asterisk or cross), while here numbers have been used.

The German text is taken from: *Herrn Alexander Popens Lockenraub, ein scherzhaftes Heldengedicht. Aus dem Englischen in deutsche Verse übersetzt, von Luisen Adelgunden Victorien Gottschedinn. Nebst einem Anhange zwoer freyen Uebersetzungen aus dem Französischen* (Leipzig: Breitkopf, 1744). The dedication to Luise Dorothea, Herzogin von Sachsen-Gotha has been omitted but all other material has been transcribed. By and large, the original orthography and punctuation have been reproduced, although a number of changes have been made. Occasionally the German text uses the character 'm̃' as an abbreviation for 'mm' or 'u.' for 'und' and the word has been written out in full here. In the German translation, characters' speech is marked with double quotation marks at the beginning of every line except for some of the utterances in Canto Five which are printed in a slightly larger bold font. The use of double quotation marks has been retained in this edition, and double quotation marks have been added in Canto Five. The German text uses various different methods in the paratexts to signal emphasis or mark quotations; here italics have been used for emphasis and single inverted commas have been used for quotations. In the footnotes, Gottsched's use of italics has been retained in instances when she quotes whole lines from the source text, and italics have also been used when she glosses lines from the French translation. Gottsched indicates footnotes through a system of asterisks and crosses, while here they are numbered.

In preparing the notes, I am indebted to the following modern editions of Pope's poem: *The Twickenham Edition of the Poems of Alexander Pope*, ed. by John Butt, 11 vols, 3rd edn (London: Methuen, 1961–69), II: *'The Rape of the Lock' and Other Poems*, ed. by Geoffrey Tillotson (1962) and Alexander Pope, *The Rape of the Lock*, ed. by Elizabeth Gurr (Oxford: Oxford University Press, 1992).

NOTES

Vorrede

prosaischen deutschen Uebersetzung — The earlier prose translation to which Gottsched refers is *Der merckwürdige Haar-Locken-Raub des Herrn Pope: Aus dem Englischen ins Deutsche übersetzt* (1739).

meinen gallischen Dollmetscher — Johann Christoph Gottsched recounted in his biography of his wife how Gottsched was later sorry to discover that the anonymous French translator on whom she here vents her spleen was in fact a family friend. The French translator was 'Herr Hofprediger von Perard' and the Gottscheds met him by chance in Stettin on a journey they undertook shortly after the publication of *Der Lockenraub*. See J. C. Gottsched, 'Leben', n. p.

einigen Herren — French Huguenots living in Germany who wrote about German letters in the *Journal littéraire de l'Allemagne, de la Suisse et du Nord*. Gottsched is referring in particular to a review article in the journal which had criticized her in passing for being too negative about the French in the prefatory material to *Zwo Schriften, das Maaß der lebendigen Kräftebetreffend* (1741), her translation of work by the French scientists Emilie du Châtelet and Jean-Jacques Dortous de Mairan. Gottsched had praised Châtelet for her support of Leibniz over Descartes and Newton in the so-called 'vis viva' debate (a scientific debate which had been raging for many years among European scholars about the force of bodies in motion), seeing it as evidence that Germany could now boast great minds who were challenging the dominance of the French in the republic of letters.

Schreiben an die Marquisinn von Chatelet — The 'Schreiben der Uebersetzerin an die Fr. Marquisinn von Chatelet' was a 120-line poem included at the beginning of Gottsched's *Zwo Schriften, das Maaß der lebendigen Kräfte betreffend* (1741).

drey Männer — the three men mentioned in the *Journal littéraire* article are Pierre-Louis Moreau de Maupertuis (1698–1759), Alexis-Claude Clairaut (1713–1765) and Delisle, the last of whom may be either the cartographer Guillaume Delisle (1625–1726) or his brother the astronomer Joseph-Nicolas Delisle (1688–1768).

Maupertuis — In 1736 Maupertuis had led an expedition to the Arctic Circle on behalf of the Parisian Académie des sciences to collect measurements which were meant to determine the shape of the earth; the Lapland team concluded that the earth was a flattened spheroid and thus the popular perception was that the expedition had confirmed the theories of Huygens and Newton. See Mary Terrall, *The Man Who Flattened the Earth: Maupertuis and the Sciences in the Enlightenment* (Chicago: University of Chicago Press, 2002), chapters 4 and 5. Gottsched was generally ill-disposed towards Maupertuis and in the early 1750s became involved in a campaign to discredit him and the position he adopted as President of the Berlin Académie des sciences in a high-profile quarrel with Johann Samuel König; this resulted in the publication of her *Sammlung aller Streitschriften, die neulich über das vorgebliche Gesetz der Natur, von der kleinsten Kraft in den Wirkungen der Körper, zwischen dem Hn. Präsidenten von Maupertuis, zu Berlin, Herrn Professor König in Holland u. a. m. gewechselt worden* (1753). For more on this affair, see Brown, *Luise Gottsched the Translator*, chapter 6.

Voltaire — Gottsched is presumably referring to Voltaire's 'Ode à Messieurs de l'Académie des Sciences, 1738, qui ont été sous l'équator et au cercle polaire mesurer des degrés de latitude' (1738).

Pater Bouhours — Dominique, père Bouhours (1628–1702) was a French Jesuit writer who had written in his *Entretiens d'Ariste et d'Eugène* (1671) that the Germans were incapable of writing poetry because of their lack of 'esprit'. The book had caused a scandal in Germany on its publication and remained in people's consciousness throughout the eighteenth century. See Max Freiherr von Waldberg, 'Eine deutsch-französische Literaturfehde', *Beiträge zur neueren Literaturgeschichte*, 16 (1930), 87–116 and Erich Haase, 'Zur Frage, ob ein Deutscher ein "bel esprit" sein kann', *Germanisch-Romanische Monatsschrift*, 9 (1959), 360–75.

Afterbrut — Gottsched is referring to the following comment in the *Journal littéraire* article: 'Il y a eu un tems où le François pensoit très injustement du mérite de ses voisins; il paroit qu'on veut lui rendre la pareille. La Postérité (je traduis aussi poliment que je puis le mot énergique d'*Afterbrut*) des grands hommes qui ont illustré le Regne de *Louis* XIV n'est pas tout à fait indigne d'eux, & ils reconnoitroient chez plusieurs de leurs neveux, leur sang, leurs talens & leur génie.' *Journal littéraire de l'Allemagne, de la Suisse et du Nord*, 2.2 (1743), 402–26 (p. 421).

Herr d'Argens — Jean-Baptiste le Boyer, marquis d'Argens (1704–1771) was a Frenchman who spent part of his life in Germany and wrote condescendingly about the Germans in his works.

Fleschier — Esprit Fléchier (1632–1710) was a French bishop who was famed for his funeral orations for the nobility; his oration on the death of Henri de la Tour d'Auvergne, vicomte de Turenne, for example, 'became an anthology piece, constantly cited by teachers of rhetoric'. See *The New Oxford Companion to Literature in French*, ed. by Peter France (Oxford: Clarendon Press, 1995), p. 819. Gottsched could be referring to Charles Frey de Neuville's funeral oration for Cardinal Fleury in 1743, which led for example to the critic Elie-Catherine Fréron publishing a *Lettre sur l'oraison funèbre du Cardinal Fleury* (1743). The debate surrounding the oration may have been familar to her because a member of the Leipzig Deutsche Gesellschaft had published a translation the previous year entitled *Des P. von Neuville Trauerrede auf den Cardinal v. Fleury, die er auf Befehl des Königs von Frankreich in Paris gehalten hat: Nebst einem Schreiben wegen dieser Rede und einer Widerlegung desselben* (1743). In the 1750s, Johann Christoph Gottsched wrote the preface for a translation of Fléchier's speeches, in which he praised Fléchier in the warmest tones and drew an unfavourable comparison with Cardinal Fleury's 'Lobredner'. See *Esprit Fleschiers Lob- und Trauerreden: Nebst dem Leben desselben von einigen Mitgliedern der königl. deutschen Gesellschaft zu Königsberg übersetzt, und mit einer Vorrede Hrn. Prof. Gottsched ans Licht gesellt von Christian Cölestin Flottweilen* (1755).

ein gewisser Schweizer — presumably the Swiss mathematician Johann Samuel König, who became Châtelet's tutor in 1739. König fell out with Châtelet when she published her *Institutions de physique* in 1740 as he claimed that the work was really his.

einer gewissen jungen Gräfinn — unclear whom Gottsched is referring to here.

Frau Wernerinn — Anna Maria Werner (1689–1753), court painter in Dresden.

Frau Deshoulieres — Antoinette du Ligier de la Garde Deshoulières (1638–1694) was the most highly regarded lyric poet of her day; in 1671 she had been awarded the Académie Française's inaugural poetry prize. See France, *The New Oxford Companion to Literature in French*, p. 234.

Canto One

Line 3 Gottsched assumes that the Baron is Henry Cromwell. She is referring to a letter of 15 July 1711 which Pope wrote to Cromwell: Cromwell had recently visited Pope in the country and the visit had been much enjoyed by all, particularly the 'Ladies'. Pope comments: 'The Trophy you bore away from one of 'em, in your Snuffbox, will doubtless preserve her Memory, and be a Testimony of your admiration, for ever' and includes eight lines of verse which anticipate *The Rape of the Lock* in both form and content. See *The Correspondence of Alexander Pope*, ed. by George Sherburn, 5 vols (Oxford: Clarendon Press, 1956), I: *1704–1718*, p. 125. Later editors assume that 'C –' refers to John Caryll, an acquaintance who apparently suggested to Pope that he should write the poem.

Line 4 Gottsched rightly identifies 'Belinda' as Miss Arabella Fermor. The Pope edition she used had been prefaced by a dedication 'To Mrs. Arabella Fermor' which makes the link between Fermor and Belinda. However, the source of her information in this note is not clear; it has never been definitely proven when and where the incident which gave rise to the poem took place. See *The Twickenham Edition of the Poems of Alexander Pope*, II, p. 81.

Line 8 Pope uses the word 'Belle' three times in the poem (I. 8, I. 10 and II. 16) and each time Gottsched translates it with 'Schöne'. This is perfectly adequate but does not convey the subtle pun: 'Belle' was a short form of 'Arabella', the name of the real-life protagonist Miss Arabella Fermor, and a Gallicism just coming into currency meaning a beautiful young woman. See *The Twickenham Edition of the Poems of Alexander Pope*, II, p. 143.

Line 13 Gottsched often opts for 'Phöbus' where Pope has 'Sol' or 'the Sun' (e.g. II. 2) or 'the sun-beams' (e.g. II. 48). This may be in part because the word is useful to her metrically; it is also highly appropriate in the context of mock-epic verse and Pope himself uses '*Phœbus*' for sun in II. 35.

Line 17 Gottsched's interpretation of the first half of this line in the footnote is probably wrong; it is more likely that Belinda is ringing her bell to summon her maid Betty. (In any case, Pope has just told us that it is noon rather than 11 o'clock.) However, this line is a good example of how Gottsched tries to mirror the rhythm of the source text.

Line 21 Gottsched adds information about the sylphs in a footnote, taken from *Le Comte de Gabalis, ou entretiens sur les sciences secretes* (1670) by Nicolas de Montfaucon de Villars which was a work she had in her library. The text had been mentioned by Pope in his dedication 'To Mrs. Arabella Fermor'.

Line 23 Gottsched's 'schöner als ein Stutzer' misses out the reference to the 'Birth-Night Beau', which evokes the dazzling outfits worn by young men attending evening festivities at Court to celebrate a Royal Birthday.

Line 30 Gottsched has swapped around the 'Nurse' and the 'Priest', making the order of the following lines less logical, as lines 31–32 refer to the teachings of the Nurse and lines 33–34 to the teachings of the Priest.

Lines 32 A rare occasion where Gottsched changes the sense of the source text, not capturing the idea of the 'silver token' (silver coins left by fairies, e.g. for baby teeth) or 'circled green' (rings on grass said to be caused by fairies dancing in a circle).

Line 44 Gottsched retains the general sense of this line but misses out the reference to the Ring, i.e. the circular track in Hyde Park around which it was fashionable to ride in a carriage.

Lines 45–46 Gottsched's 'Gefolge' is not a precise rendering of 'Equipage', which denotes 'A carriage and horses, with attendant footmen' (OED) but she captures the sense; she has changed the reference to 'two Pages and a Chair' (i.e. sedan chair) to 'Kutsch und Pferd mit zween blanken Edelknaben', but may have done so because of her need for extra syllables.

Line 50 Pope's 'Vehicles' is a pun referring back to the 'Equipage' in line 45; this subtlety is not carried across in the translation.

Line 89 'falsches Schamroth' is a good translation of 'bidden blush', which refers to cheeks made-up with rouge.

Lines 97–98 Gottsched substitues Damon and Thirsis for Pope's Florio and Damon. Florio and Damon were apparently common names for lovers in light verse — see Gurr, *The Rape of the Lock*, p. 35. Gottsched appears to have inserted a more concrete reference to the lovers Damon and Lydia (Thirsis) who appear in Horace's odes.

Line 138 Gottsched captures the satire in this line by slipping the incongruous 'Bibel' in amongst the trivial items on Belinda's dressing-table. Note that Pope has 'Bibles' in the plural while Gottsched uses the singular form: small attractively bound Bibles were commonly found in the possession of young ladies in early eighteenth-century England, who may have received several as gifts, but presumably these small Bibles were not fashionable in Germany. While the general sense of this line is conveyed to German readers, it is not as poetic as the original, being less alliterative and not reflecting the way Pope chooses a one-syllable word followed by two-syllable words and ends with a trisyllable.

Lines 143–44 Belinda is applying rouge to her cheeks ('purer blush') and some form of cosmetics to her eyes ('keener lightening'), perhaps the juice of deadly nightshade, known as belladonna, which would have enlarged her pupils; this is implied too in Gottsched's translation in the use of 'geläutert' and 'schärfre'. See *The Twickenham Edition of the Poems of Alexander Pope*, II, p. 157.

Line 148 'Betty' was a standard name in English literature of the time for a lady's maid; Gottsched substitutes 'Sylvia' instead, perhaps for the sake of the metre.

Canto Two

Line 7 Gottsched's rendition of 'a sparking Cross' as 'ein Kreuz von großem Werth' does not convey the suggestion that the cross may be bejewelled and thus worn by Belinda as an ornament in order to draw attention to herself (or her bosom). But the German phrase could imply that Belinda is wearing the cross to display her wealth, thus hinting too at ostentation.

Line 8 Mauschel, derived from Mausche (Moses), was a term used to denote Jews.

Lines 33–34 In the source text, these lines convey criticism of society as a whole ('Few ask ...') whereas Gottsched's criticism is more specifically directed at lovers.

Line 40 'Siegeszeichen' for 'trophies' nicely reproduces Pope's mock-epic language.

Line 47 In the source text, 'painted vessel' seems to suggest both the boat on which Belinda is travelling down the Thames, and Belinda herself; Gottsched's choice of the more specific noun 'Fahrzeug' means that the second meaning is perhaps lost.

Lines 55–57 The sibilants in the source text, which evoke the sound of the flying sylphs, are not reproduced in the translation.

Line 56 Gottsched retains the military language which runs though this section of the source text (cf. 'Hört, was euer Haupt befiehlt' for 'to your chief give ear' in line 73).

Lines 99–100 The references to a 'Flounce' and a 'Furbelow' — pieces of material gathered and sewn to women's clothes for decoration — are made clear to readers of the translation by the addition of 'eine neue Mode' in line 99.

Line 105 Gottsched changes 'break Diana's law', i.e. lose one's chastity, to 'irgend eins von *Dianens* Grundgesetzen' in the plural which is less explicit. In general, Gottsched tones down or omits sexual innuendos, presumably wary of social proprieties or the censors. One of Gottsched's contemporaries, the poet Friedrich von Hagedorn, certainly thought that Gottsched was acting here according to social expectations. As Gottsched's husband wrote in her biography, Hagedorn often noted 'daß an einigen schlüpfrigen Stellen, die Pope mit einfließen lassen, die Uebersetzerinn augenscheinlich nicht aus Unwissenheit, sondern aus einer ihrem Geschlechte und den guten Sitten hochanständigen Bescheidenheit, von dem Grundtext abgewichen sey'. See J. C. Gottsched, 'Leben', n. p.

Lines 107–09 Good examples of where Gottsched mirrors Pope's use of zeugma (and adds an extra one in line 108), a device employed in the poem to highlight the confused or perverse values of eighteenth-century fashionable society (cf. III. 5–6).

Line 113 Gottsched correctly identifies 'Drops' as earrings (probably diamonds).

Lines 119–20 A rare occasion where the translation retains the sexual innuendo (see note to line 105 above).

Line 133 Gottsched has either misunderstood the reference to the 'whirling Mill', or felt it would be lost on her readers. The mill was a pot used to make drinking chocolate: it contained cocoa nut powder and hot water, which was stirred with a stick inserted though the lid to make it froth. See Gurr, *The Rape of the Lock*, p. 44.

Canto Three

Lines 7–8 Gottsched expands the phrase 'great ANNA!', turning it into '*Anna*, groß zu Land und See', presumably for the purposes of metre and rhyme. Line 8 is one occasion where she does not manage to retain the zeugma.

Lines 9–10 Untypically, Gottsched deviates somewhat from the source text here, presumably because of the constraints of her verse form, although she does retain the basic sense of the original.

Line 14 Gottsched does well to identify an '*Indian* screen' as a fire-screen. She adds the reference to 'Sumatra', the Indonesian island which had been an English trading post since the early seventeenth century. Sumatra seems to have been regarded at one point as 'the Emporium of Eastern riches, whither the traders of the West resorted with their cargoes, to exchange them for the precious merchandize of the Indian Archipelago'. See William Marsden, *The History of Sumatra, Containing an Account of the Government, Laws, Customs and Manners of the Native Inhabitants, with a Description of the Natural Productions and a Relation of the Ancient Political State of that Island*, 2nd edn (London: Printed for the Author, 1784), p. iii.

Line 26 There is some suggestion in the source text that Belinda may experience the card game as a kind of sexual encounter, as hinted at here ('burns to encounter') and in line 28 ('swells her breast'). This language is not carried across in the translation.

Line 31 Gottsched may have misunderstood this line, as she translates 'hand' literally rather than the sense of 'a hand of cards'.

Line 46 In the source text, this line parodies Genesis I.v.3 ('And God said, "Let there be light" and there was light'), continuing the imagery relating to religion and religious ritual which runs through the poem and mocking here the way Belinda is viewed (or views herself) as a goddess. The German line does not echo Genesis ('Und Gott sprach: Es werde Licht! Und es ward Licht') in the same way.

Lines 49–53 Spadillio (the ace of spades), Manillio (the two of spades) and Basto (the ace of clubs) become female in the translation, as these are female nouns in German. Veronica C. Richel believes that 'the distinctly masculine character of the war is sacrificed' and that these lines are symptomatic of the 'failure of the

German rendition to capture the tumult and excitement of the fray'. See Richel, 'Luise Gottsched's *Der Lockenraub*', pp. 482–83.

Line 62 Gottsched seems to make a clever substitution of 'Scherwenzel' for 'Lu'. In Lu (a.k.a. Lanterloo or Loo) Pam, the Knave of Clubs, is the top trumping card; in 'Scherwenzel' the lower ranking cards seem also to be the most powerful. See Johann-Christoph Adelung, *Versuch eines vollständigen grammatisch-kritischen Wörterbuches der Hochdeutschen Mundart* (Leipzig: Breitkopf, 1774–86), IV (1780), col. 39.

Line 106 Gottsched's interpretation of this line is logical but in the source text 'crackle' probably refers to the sound of the berries being roasted in a chafing dish before being ground in a mill. See Gurr, *The Rape of the Lock*, p. 50.

Line 107 The source text may have been misunderstood here: 'shining Altars of Japan' probably refers to lacquered tables or cabinets imported from Japan, which were very fashionable in England at this time. See Gurr, *The Rape of the Lock*, p. 50.

Line 110 Gottsched has changed the reference to '*China*'s earth' (i.e. the coffee cups) to 'Japans Thon', establishing a link back to line 107.

Lines 117–18 Pope is satirizing the amateur politicians who frequented London's coffee houses: a well-known phenomenon held up for derision in the popular moral weeklies (see *The Twickenham Edition of the Poems of Alexander Pope*, II, p. 176). The lines are rendered faithfully in the translation but presumably would not have had quite the same resonance for German readers.

Line 152 The note on this line in the source text, referring the reader to *Paradise Lost*, is expanded by Gottsched: she uses the opportunity to be critical of Milton, an author famously rejected by the Gottsched school for his wild imagination. Compare the comparison of Homer with Milton, and further criticism of Milton, in the note on IV. 51.

Line 165 Pope is alluding in the source text to Delariviere Manley's *Secret Memoirs and Manners of Several Persons of Quality, of Both Sexes: From the New Atalantis, an Island in the Mediterranean* (1709), a political satire which was a *succès de scandale* and widely read in Britain at the time Pope wrote his poem but probably unfamiliar to readers in Germany in the 1740s; in the translation '*Atalantis*' evokes more generally the ancient myth.

Canto Four

Line 17 The alliteration in the German line nicely echoes that in the source text.

Lines 29–30 The 'store of pray'rs' in the source text has become a reference to Michael Cubach's *Einer gläubigen und andächtigen Seelen täglichen Bet-, Buß-, Lob- und Danck-Opffer, d.i. ein groß vollkommnes Gebet-Buch* (1654), which was 'the most popular collection of prayers of its day' [and] remained 'very popular in the eighteenth century, [reaching] twenty-seven editions by 1791'. See Nicholas Hope, *German and Scandinavian Protestantism 1700–1918* (Oxford: Clarendon Press, 1995), p. 31.

Lines 43–46 In the source text these lines refer to optical illusions created on stage; Gottsched may have missed this, although she does recognize that 'Angels in machines' (line 46) belong in the theatre.

Line 54 In the German translation, this line is no longer sexually explicit.

Line 69 Gottsched has changed the reference to 'Citron-waters' (an alcoholic drink), perhaps misunderstanding the source text.

Line 109 The sense of this line is captured well in the translation: at the time a 'toast' could denote 'a celebrated woman whose health is often drunk' (Samuel Johnson, quoted in *The Twickenham Edition of the Poems of Alexander Pope*, II, p. 192).

Lines 117–18 The London references in these lines prove difficult for the translator. Gottsched's solution in line 117 is puzzling (the 'Circus' being the circular drive referred to in the source text in I. 44 which was notorious for its dusty air) but she finds a clever alternative in line 118. The 'Bow' refers to the church of St Mary-le-Bow in the City of London and was not the usual stamping ground of the fashionable set: 'Being born within the sound of Bow bells identified one as a local, as opposed to the more fashionable West End where wits would expect to live.' See Gurr, *The Rape of the Lock*, p. 59.

Lines 123–24 Gottsched renders the general sense of these lines but alters some of the details. For example, 'to cloud' — as in 'clouded cane' — seems to have meant at the time to 'variegate with dark veins' (Samuel Johnson, quoted in *The Twickenham Edition of the Poems of Alexander Pope*, II, p. 194).

Line 156 Gottsched changes the reference to 'Bohea' (tea) to 'Caffe', perhaps considering it to be too obscure for German readers.

Line 176 Gottsched changes the last line of the canto, omitting the sexual innuendo.

Canto Five

Line 40 Gottsched correctly identifies 'whalebones' as being those used to stiffen petticoats. 'Fischbein-Rocke' had been in the title of one of her earlier works, *Die Pietisterey im Fischbein-Rocke, oder Die doctormäßige Frau: in einem Lustspiel vorgestellt* (1736), a translation of Guillaume-Hyacinthe Bougeant's *La Femme docteur ou la théologie tombée en quenouille* (1730).

Line 42 Pope's 'base, and treble voices' become 'Baß, Discant und Mittelstimm', which does not fit so well in this description of the battle of the sexes, but Gottsched has presumably added an extra noun for the sake of the metre.

Line 44 'Mortal' in the source text has two possible meanings: on the one hand it suggests lethal wounds (and allows Pope to draw a wry comparison with warriors in the epics) and on the other wounds inflicted by humans (which ties in with the imagery of the battle of the sexes). Only the first sense is carried across in the translation.

Line 47 '*Majens* Sohn' is another way of referring to Hermes: Hermes is the son of Maia, one of the Pleiades.

Line 53 Gottsched has found a good alternative to the phrase 'on a sconce's height', a sconce being a bracket candlestick which was hung on a wall and often had a mirror behind it.

Lines 77–78 Typically, Gottsched omits the sexual innuendo in these lines (cf. V. 97–98).

Line 105 In her note on this line, Gottsched takes the opportunity to express criticism of Shakespeare and of English drama in general. The Leipzigers were famously derided in Lessing's Seventeenth *Literaturbrief* for their dismissive attitude towards Shakespeare; in fact they had given careful consideration to the reasons why they could not advocate Shakespeare as a model for their theatrical reforms. See Robert R. Heitner, 'A Gottschedian Reply to Lessing's Seventeenth *Literaturbrief*', in *Studies in Germanic Languages and Literatures in Memory of Fred O. Nolte*, ed. by Erich Hofacker and Liselotte Dieckmann (St Louis: Washington University Press, 1963), pp. 43–58.

Line 133 Gottsched leaves out the allusion to the Mall, in Pope's time a popular spot for the fashionable set who would take walks or go for drives there.

Line 136 Gottsched adds a note on '*Rosamunder See*', i.e. Rosamond's Pond in St James's Park. She does not give the source of her information, but her comment is corroborated in various accounts, e.g. 'its secluded situation is said to have tempted a greater number of persons to commit suicide, especially unfortunate females, than any other place in London'. J. Heneage Jesse, *London: Its Celebrated Characters and Remarkable Places*, 3 vols (London: Bentley, 1871), I, 132.

BIBLIOGRAPHY

Adelung, Johann-Christoph, *Versuch eines vollständigen grammatisch-kritischen Wörterbuches der Hochdeutschen Mundart* (Leipzig: Breitkopf, 1774–86)

[Anon.] Unsigned review of *La Belle Wolfienne*, by Johann Heinrich Samuel Formey, in *Journal littéraire de l'Allemagne, de la Suisse et du Nord*, 2.2 (1743), 402–26

[Anon.] Unsigned review of *Herrn Alexander Popens Lockenraub*, trans. by Luise Gottsched, in *Freymüthige Nachrichten von neuen Büchern, und andern zur Gelehrtheit gehörigen Sachen*, 1 (1744), 278–80 and 283–86

[Anon.] Unsigned review of *Herrn Alexander Popens Lockenraub*, trans. by Luise Gottsched, in *Göttingische Zeitung von gelehrten Sachen*, 6 (1744), 531–32

[Anon.], Unsigned review of *Herrn Alexander Popens Lockenraub*, trans. by Luise Gottsched, in *Zuverläßige Nachrichten von dem gegenwärtigen Zustande, Veränderung und Wachsthum der Wissenschaften*, 63 (1745), 219–28

Ball, Gabriele, *Moralische Küsse: Gottsched als Zeitschriftenherausgeber und literarischer Vermittler* (Göttingen: Wallstein, 2000)

Brown, Hilary, 'Luise Gottsched the Satirist', *Modern Language Review*, 103 (2008), 1036–50

Brown, Hilary, *Luise Gottsched the Translator* (Rochester, NY: Camden House, 2012)

Fabian, Bernhard, 'English Books and their Eighteenth-Century German Readers', in *The Widening Circle: Essays on the Circulation of Literature in Eighteenth-Century Europe*, ed. by Paul J. Korshin (Philadelphia: University of Pennsylvania Press, 1976), pp. 119–96

France, Peter (ed.), *The New Oxford Companion to Literature in French* (Oxford: Clarendon Press, 1995)

Goodman, Katherine R., *Amazons and Apprentices: Women and the German Parnassus in the Early Enlightenment* (Rochester, NY: Camden House, 1999)

Gottsched, Johann Christoph, 'Catalogue de la Bibliotheque Choisie, de Feue Madame Gottsched, née Kulmus, proprement reliée en veau doré, et autres relieures Angloises, et Italiennes', in Luise Gottsched, *Sämmtliche kleinere Gedichte* (Leipzig: Breitkopf, 1763), pp. 487–532

——, 'Leben der weil. hochedelgebohrnen, nunmehr sel. Frau Luise Adelgunde Victoria Gottschedinn', in Luise Gottsched, *Sämmtliche kleinere Gedichte* (Leipzig: Breitkopf, 1763), n. p.

——, *Briefwechsel: Unter Einschluß des Briefwechsels von Luise Adelgunde Victorie Gottsched*, ed. by Detlef Döring and others, 25 vols (Berlin: de Gruyter, 2007–)

Gottsched, Luise (trans.) *Herrn Alexander Popens Lockenraub: Ein scherzhaftes Heldengedicht. Aus dem Englischen in deutsche Verse übersetzt, von Luisen Adelgunden Victorien Gottschedinn. Nebst einem Anhange zwoer freyen Uebersetzungen aus dem Französischen* (Leipzig: Breitkopf, 1744)

—— (trans.), *Der engländische Guardian oder Aufseher*, 2 vols (Leipzig: Breitkopf, 1749)

[——], Review of *Sieg des Liebesgottes. Eine Nachahmung des popischen Lockenraubes*, by Johann Peter Uz, *Das Neueste aus der anmuthigen Gelehrsamkeit*, 3 (1753), 239–40

——, *Briefe*, ed. by Dorothea von Runckel, 3 vols (Dresden: Harpeter, 1771–72)

—— (trans.), *Herrn Alexander Popens Lockenraub: Ein scherzhaftes Heldengedicht. Aus dem Englischen in deutsche Verse übersetzet von Luisen Adelgunden Victorien Gottschedinn. In dieser zweyten Auflage durchaus verbessert, und beynahe ganz umgearbeitet* (Leipzig: Breitkopf, 1772)

Gurr, Elizabeth (ed.), *Alexander Pope, 'The Rape of the Lock'* (Oxford: Oxford University Press, 1992)

Haase, Erich, 'Zur Frage, ob ein Deutscher ein "bel esprit" sein kann', *Germanisch-Romanische Monatsschrift*, 9 (1959), 360–75

Heinzelmann, J. H., 'Pope in Germany in the Eighteenth Century', *Modern Philology*, 10 (1913), 317–64

Heitner, Robert R., 'A Gottschedian Reply to Lessing's Seventeenth *Literaturbrief*', in *Studies in Germanic Languages and Literatures in Memory of Fred O. Nolte*, ed. by Erich Hofacker and Liselotte Dieckmann (St Louis: Washington University Press, 1963), pp. 43–58

Hope, Nicholas, *German and Scandinavian Protestantism 1700–1918* (Oxford: Clarendon Press, 1995)

Höschele, Eleonora, 'Von "gunst zur wahrheit angetrieben": Leben und Werk der Dresdner Hofzeichnerin Anna Maria Werner', *Jahrbuch der Staatlichen Kunstsammlungen Dresden*, 28 (2000), 33–46

Inbar, Eva Maria, 'Zum Englischstudium im Deutschland des XVIII. Jahrhunderts', *Arcadia: Zeitschrift für vergleichende Literaturwissenschaft*, 15 (1980), 14–28

Jesse, J. Heneage, *London: Its Celebrated Characters and Remarkable Places*, 3 vols (London: Bentley, 1871)

Krebs, Roland, '*Les Lettres françaises et germaniques* de Mauvillon et leur réception en Allemagne', *Dix-Huitième Siècle*, 14 (1982), 377–90

——, 'La France jugée par Gottsched: ennemie héréditaire ou modèle culturel?', *Revue d'Allemagne*, 18 (1986), 585–99

Marsden, William, *The History of Sumatra, Containing an Account of the Government, Laws, Customs and Manners of the Native Inhabitants, with a Description of the Natural Productions and a Relation of the Ancient Political State of that Island*, 2nd edn (London: Printed for the Author, 1784)

Oppel, Horst, *Englisch-deutsche Literaturbeziehungen*, Grundlagen der Anglistik und Amerikanistik, 1–2, 2 vols (Berlin: Schmidt, 1971)

Petzet, Erich, 'Die deutschen Nachahmungen des Popeschen *Lockenraubes*', *Zeitschrift für vergleichende Literaturgeschichte*, 4 (1891), 409–33

Pope, Alexander, *The Works of Alexander Pope, Esq.: With Explanatory Notes and Additions Never Before Printed*, 4 vols (London: Lintot, 1736)

——, *The Correspondence of Alexander Pope*, ed. by George Sherburn, 5 vols (Oxford: Clarendon Press, 1956)

——, *The Twickenham Edition of the Poems of Alexander Pope*, ed. by John Butt, 11 vols, 3rd edn (London: Methuen, 1961–69), II: *'The Rape of the Lock' and Other Poems*, ed. by Geoffrey Tillotson (1962)

Price, Lawrence Marsden, *English Literature in Germany*, University of California

Publications in Modern Philology, 37 (Berkeley: University of California Press, 1957)

RICHEL, VERONICA C., *Luise Gottsched: A Reconsideration* (Bern: Peter Lang, 1973)

——, 'Luise Gottsched's *Der Lockenraub* and Alexander Pope's *The Rape of the Lock*: A Comparative Analysis', *Neuphilologische Mitteilungen*, 3 (1975), 473–87

TERRALL, MARY, *The Man Who Flattened the Earth: Maupertuis and the Sciences in the Enlightenment* (Chicago: University of Chicago Press, 2002)

WALDBERG, MAX FREIHERR VON, 'Eine deutsch-französische Literaturfehde', *Beiträge zur neueren Literaturgeschichte*, 16 (1930), 87–116

WANIEK, GUSTAV, *Gottsched und die deutsche Litteratur seiner Zeit* (Leipzig: Breitkopf und Härtel, 1897; repr. Leipzig: Zentralantiquariat der DDR, 1972)

WEHR, MARIANNE, 'Johann Christoph Gottscheds Briefwechsel: Ein Beitrag zur Geschichte der deutschen Frühaufklärung' (unpublished doctoral thesis, University of Leipzig, 1965)

WOODMAN, THOMAS, 'Alexander Pope', in *Reader's Guide to Literature in English*, ed. by Mark Hawkins-Dady (London: Fitzroy Dearborn, 1996), pp. 605–07

MHRA European Translations

The guiding principle of this series is to make available translations that had a significant impact on the receiving culture at the time of their publication, but that are now either completely or relatively inaccessible. Aimed at an academic market, titles in this series will also reflect current areas of scholarly debate and/or topics studied on undergraduate and postgraduate courses.

Each volume will include a substantial introduction, and textual and explanatory notes. The introduction will describe the ways in which this particular translation (or these translations) shaped literary and/or intellectual currents in the receiving culture, and will provide a coherently argued account of the omissions and distortions of the translation/s.

Titles will be selected by members of the Editorial Board and edited by leading academics.

Alison Finch
General Editor

Editorial Board

Published titles

1. *Böece de Confort remanié. Edition critique.*
   (Glynnis M. Cropp, 2011)
2. *Luise Gottsched, Der Lockenraub/*
   Alexander Pope, The Rape of the Lock
   (Hilary Brown, 2014)
3. *Pedro Calderón de la Barca, 'La devoción de la cruz'/*
   August Wilhelm Schlegel, 'Die Andacht zum Kreuze'.
   (Carol Tully, 2012)

For details of how to order please visit our website at:
www.translations.mhra.org.uk

www.ingramcontent.com/pod-product-compliance
Ingram Content Group UK Ltd.
Pitfield, Milton Keynes, MK11 3LW, UK
UKHW021113200726
13857UKWH00003B/1216